RABBIT HASH KENTUCKY

★RIVER BORN, KENTUCKY BRED★

DONALD CLARE

THE History PRESS

Published by The History Press
Charleston, SC 29403
www.historypress.net

Front cover, top right: The original round photograph of the Wilson and Riddell general store taken by nineteenth-century historian Reuben Gold Thwaites in 1894 during his travels down the Ohio River from Redstone to Cairo. His travel journal and photographs were later the basis for his book *Afloat on the Ohio*, published in 1897 and republished in 1903 under the title *On the Storied Ohio. Photograph used with permission from the Wisconsin State Historical Society.*

First published 2012

Manufactured in the United States

ISBN 978.1.60949.435.3

Library of Congress CIP data applied for.

In each case, had it not been for the passion and initiative of one long-forgotten individual, this country would not be blessed with the extant preservation of such historically and culturally important and significant places as Mount Vernon or Monticello. Rabbit Hash, Kentucky, is no exception.

This book is respectfully dedicated to Louie Scott, who saved Rabbit Hash "one piece at a time."

CONTENTS

PREFACE

As of late, finding one's ancestors and roots has become all the rage, so to speak. Genealogy has become the latest pastime and industry on the World Wide Web and in social media, and a lot of folks seem to be taking an interest in something that heretofore was limited to their parents' or grandparents' family bibles.

Important ingredients of this search for *who* you are include *where* you came from and *how* you got there. People laugh when they are told that the population of Rabbit Hash, Kentucky, is one. That's right, one person lives in the town of Rabbit Hash. But hundreds upon hundreds of others claim to live there, and thousands upon thousands can trace their family roots back to this small Ohio River hamlet in rural Boone County, Kentucky.

For generations, Rabbit Hash has claimed a certain kind of fame and notoriety that other small towns can't. Obviously, this is due to the name of the town, and that will all be explained in the following pages. This name has been repeated tongue-in-cheek by authors, journalists, newspaper reporters, television and movie personalities, advertising people, musicians and persons of every other walk of life looking for that quick chuckle or smile. Since 1919, the Rabbit Hash General Store has been a backdrop of Coca-Cola advertising. Don't think that other soft-drink brands haven't coveted that distinction, either! During the Korean War, Bob Hope opened several of his USO shows for the troops with "Greetings from Rabbit Hash, Kentucky." Charles Kuralt wandered through once and did a piece on the town. Most recently, CBS's Bill Geist devoted one of his *Sunday Morning* news shows to covering the mayoral election taking place in Rabbit Hash during the national elections of 2008. He even asked Bob Schieffer's opinion and prediction of that celebrated mayoral race. Hollywood producer Jude Prest and LifeLike Productions made a full-length documentary movie about Rabbit Hash and its unusual races for town mayor, and there was even a follow-up Animal Planet segment entitled *Mayor Dog*. You see, the past three elected mayors of this town have been dogs (actual canines). Robert Redford stopped in the store one Sunday morning to buy Rabbit Hash T-shirts and coffee mugs. No one saw him in town except the store clerk and one other older tourist couple, but it was definitely him. It seems he had been down to the Keeneland Horse Sales in Lexington and was driving back to the Greater Cincinnati International Airport for his flight back home. He said a few of his friends back home had Rabbit Hash T-shirts, and he wanted one, too.

In the early 1980s, a local Cincinnati radio station invented a spoof about a winery in Rabbit Hash, Kentucky, which continued for more than a year. It supposedly was operating underneath the store and was called the Hiney Winery, run by the brothers Thor and Big Red. It attracted so many people that the store proprietor had to come up with a brand of Rabbit Hash–labeled beer to sell to the visitors (beer because the store had a beer license; obtaining a liquor or wine license would have been almost impossible at that time). In 1984, parts of the PBS movie *The Adventures of Huckleberry Finn* were filmed in town as Rabbit Hash was turned into a movie set.

The town of Rabbit Hash was transformed into the set for several scenes of the PBS movie *The Adventures of Huckleberry Finn* back in 1984. The General Store became a nineteenth-century Mississippi River mercantile operation. *From the Rabbit Hash Historical Society collection.*

A scene from the PBS film *The Adventures of Huckleberry Finn* showing "the Duke" pitching the values of phrenology to the townsfolk from the porch of the converted Rabbit Hash General Store, 1984. *From the Rabbit Hash Historical Society collection.*

Many other stories like these abound. The popularity of the name Rabbit Hash is international. A German television commercial for Kentucky Fried Chicken was once filmed here, but it would never have been allowed to air in the United States. It was almost borderline pornographic or at least X-rated. It was a sure reminder that European television accepts much more risqué scenery than its U.S. counterpart. Recently, Rabbit Hash was voted one of the top ten funniest town names in the *world* by SmarterTravel.com! On and on it goes, but one thing is certain: Rabbit Hash, Kentucky, is an example of the importance and significance of every small town and community in our country. Its history is *our* history, and it is our responsibility—and should also be considered our privilege—to see that this history is recorded and preserved.

INTRODUCTION

Rabbit Hash, Kentucky. Now who in his right mind would ever name a town or community Rabbit Hash? That is just plain foolishness. No doubt, it was just a silly prank conjured up by some sort of hippie cult, rebelling against any and every authority possible and having no respect whatsoever for the proud commonwealth of Kentucky, much less for this great country of ours. It was surely a hallucinogenic epiphany of some longhaired Vietnam War protestor back in 1968 or '69.

No, not quite. Take a hard left at Big Bone Lick and go back at least 130 years. It was in 1879 that this little Ohio River hamlet in western Boone County, Kentucky, was officially named. Besides that, it was given its own post office, having the same authority, function and official governmental sanction as the New York, Chicago or Cincinnati Post Offices. Yes, Uncle Sam recognized Rabbit Hash, Kentucky, as an official U.S. town way back then. At that same time, the U.S. flag had only thirty-eight stars. In other words, Rabbit Hash, Kentucky, predates the states of Idaho, Montana, New Mexico, North Dakota, Oklahoma, South Dakota, Utah, Washington and Wyoming.

In order to make this tale just a little more unbelievable, the local folks were calling the Carlton Magisterial District by the name of Rabbit Hash as far back as 1847 or thereabouts. This section of western Boone County was included in the official voting district designated by the name Carlton, taken from a local landowner/settler on the banks of the Ohio River, across from Rising Sun, Indiana. Well, it just so happened that thirty-nine miles farther downriver was the town of Carrollton, Kentucky, also situated on the banks

Besides the town of Rabbit Hash, there are other small communities in proximity having equally curious and (now) famous names. They, too, at one time had their own post offices and general stores. Shown here is a postcard offering addressed to someone in Beaver Lick, Kentucky, and postmarked from Big Bone, Kentucky. *From the author's personal collection.*

A letter postmarked from the Beaver Lick, Kentucky post office in 1920. *From the author's personal collection.*

of the Ohio River. It doesn't take a steamboat scientist to figure out that Carlton's mail was being dropped off in Carrollton and vice versa, creating a huge dilemma for the local postal authorities. Since Carrollton antedated Carlton and had a much larger population, Uncle Sam placed the name-changing ultimatum on the shoulders of the Carlton inhabitants.

It was a no-brainer. The locals had been calling their little river hamlet Rabbit Hash for at least thirty years. They were having all their mail posted to Rising Sun, Indiana, anyway, because it was much easier to simply cross the river at that time than it was to travel to Carrollton by river or land to retrieve their mail. The unofficial name of Rabbit Hash goes back as far as 1847. That was the year of an Ohio River flood of fairly major proportions, one that removed homes, barns, livestock and stored crops from their rightful locations to areas much farther downriver. As the townsfolk helplessly watched the devastation and destruction, they lamented to one another how horrible and unfair Mother Nature had become to subject these God-fearing, self-sustaining yeoman farmers to a travesty and tragedy of such biblical proportions.

This flood occurred sometime between Thanksgiving and Christmas. "Oh, what will we do? The waters have taken our fattened goose and our prime hog. What shall we do for our holiday feasts and celebrations?" the local women complained, forlorn and despairing.

"Why, my dear ladies, do not despair and worry your precious selves over such trivial matters! As you can see, we will indeed have plenty of rabbit hash for our holiday feasts!" And with that, Frank, the town jester and imbiber of everything alcoholic, commenced shooting rabbits as the floodwaters drove them farther inland and upland.

Sure enough, the whole community survived the 1847 flood and enjoyed an ample supply of rabbit meat to sustain it through that particular ordeal. At that point, the townsfolk began to refer to Frank as "Rabbit Hash." Eventually, that individual moniker became the colloquial name for that small agrarian river community throughout the 1850s and '60s. By the end of the Civil War, Rabbit Hash was well established as the small Kentucky town opposite Rising Sun, Indiana.

Now, Rabbit Hash was really no different from any other small rural agrarian Ohio River community in Kentucky back then, and there were a lot of them. But it *was* different! There was just something about Rabbit Hash that made it seem unlike other places. No one has ever been able to put a finger on that "thing," but it obviously has something to do with the name. Just by uttering the name out loud, something soothing happens to

A historical marker in downtown Rabbit Hash, Kentucky. *Photograph courtesy of Callie Clare.*

you—almost euphoric yet not overwhelming or life changing. It's like your psyche just snickered for a second or two and your blood pressure suddenly dropped a bit. This is not some modern pop culture phenomenon that cycles the Internet or is plagiarized in blogs. It has been documented in the literature ever since the late nineteenth century. Rabbit Hash has been described as "idyllic," "lost to time," "riverine Nirvana," "Boone's (County) piece of heaven" and other such similes of superbity.

In his 1897 *Afloat on the Ohio*, Reuben Gold Thwaites stated that Rabbit Hash "is a crude hamlet of a hundred souls, lying nestled in a green amphitheater." Presently, there are ninety-nine fewer souls living in the town itself but thousands within that green amphitheater. R.E. Banta, in his 1949 *The Ohio*, wrote:

> *Today there are no sizable cities on the river for fifty miles below Cincinnati, although early real estate promoters and town planners were no doubt optimistic of the prospects when they christened Aurora and Rising Sun on the north bank. (Whoever laid out the Kentucky town opposite Rising Sun was perhaps not so hopeful of its prosperity and growth or he would not have named it Rabbit Hash.)*

The town proper of Rabbit Hash, as of 2012, has a population of one. Just one person living in town full time! Yet people within a ten- or fifteen-mile radius claim to live in Rabbit Hash. You can address a letter to Rabbit Hash and choose one of two different zip codes, 41092 for the Union, Kentucky side of Rabbit Hash or 41005 for the Burlington, Kentucky side. The two postal jurisdictions abut each other right on the downriver Rabbit Hash National Register District boundary line.

1

EARLY SETTLEMENT PATTERNS IN BOONE COUNTY

Ever since the retreating ice from the last Pleistocene-era glacier over twelve thousand years ago began to transform the North American landscape into that with which we are now familiar, its runoff gave birth to a new drainage that we know as the Ohio River. As humans crossed over into this continent via the Beringia land bridge from Asia, they migrated down the very same corridor that the grazing Pleistocene mammals followed—the former in pursuit of meat, the latter in pursuit of grasses. Besides food, they both needed water. So they stayed in proximity to this newly formed river. These first inhabitants were called Paleo-Indians, and they were chiefly nomadic hunters who traveled in small groups.

Next came the Archaic Indians from 8000 to 1000 BC. They also hunted meat as a food source but complemented it with the gathering of nuts and edible plants. Thus, they were termed hunter-gatherers. They made their homes and villages along the Ohio River and also on the uplands for fall and winter quarters. The majority of prehistoric stone artifacts along the river in the Rabbit Hash and East Bend areas are of the Archaic culture. They did not plant or raise crops. They were the developers of the atlatl, a hand-held device used for throwing shafted spears with more speed, force and velocity, thus improving their hunting advantage.

The next prehistoric native Indian group was the Woodland people. They, too, subsisted on hunting game and gathering plants and nuts. They also fished and seined. Besides having those subsistence modalities, they also raised their own primitive gardens and grew squash and gourds. Since they did not wander as much hunting food, they had a more sedentary and stationary lifestyle, keeping to one place. The Woodland people were the first to work with pottery using local clay. At first, they hunted with spears and stone points, but later, about AD 700, they adopted the bow and arrow for hunting small game. The Woodland culture was the first to build burial mounds. In Boone County, there were numerous Adena mounds. Adena is merely a subgroup of the Woodland tradition. Hopewell is another subgroup, and they lived mainly upriver on the right bank (Ohio). The Hopewell also built burial mounds and geometric earthworks. The Woodland people carried on a fairly extensive trade network with other groups of native people located in other areas of the continent. This explains the presence of copper, marine shells, obsidian, mica and other exotic raw materials found at Woodland sites.

The next group is the Late Prehistoric, beginning around AD 1000 and continuing almost until the European contact period. They also hunted, gathered nuts and plants and tended gardens. They were really the very first farmers. Besides growing squash and gourds, they also cultivated corn and beans. They lived in permanent villages in huts made of a framework of posts dug into the ground and the roof and walls covered with bark. A hole in the peak of the roof allowed for enough ventilation for a fire to be built inside the house for heat, cooking and light. They also made ceramic pots, jars, pans and other vessels. They evaporated salt water from local salt springs in shallow ceramic saltpans to produce salt for their diets. Their villages were generally located in proximity to a water source—in this case, the Ohio River—and this is where they grew their crops. Their homes were built in a circle around a central plaza area. They buried their dead either in a cemetery area or in a small mound of earth. The town of Petersburg, just upriver from Rabbit Hash, is built on one such prehistoric Fort Ancient village site, superimposed on another earlier Fort Ancient village.

The Fort Ancient people also surrounded their villages with stockade-like fences and were the people who developed and used the small, thin, triangular chert points for their arrows. The Fort Ancient people are probably the ancestors of the Indians encountered by the first Europeans to arrive in this area. But when this did occur, the Indian population here was drastically reduced from its former numbers. No one knows for sure what happened between the time of the final days of the Fort Ancients in the 1500s and 1600s and the appearance of the white man, but the native inhabitants here all but disappeared. Most scholars have ruled out warfare, famine, pestilence or natural disasters to account for their paucity and generally agree that it was European diseases that wiped out the native inhabitants because they had no natural immunity to the many, many illnesses carried downriver by the encroaching European culture.

So who were these disease-carrying Europeans? And who really discovered the Ohio River and Rabbit Hash? Obviously, the Ohio River was first discovered by the first small band of Paleo-Indians who were following the Pleistocene megafauna down the center of this continent during the retreating stages of the last glacier, twelve thousand years ago, which accounted for the formation of what would be called the Ohio River. The arrival of the European explorers merely opens up the next chapter of the story.

The real debate of discovery and ownership of the Ohio was between France and England. Both claimed possession at one time or another and sometimes at the same time. This debate finally culminated in the French and Indian War (1754), as it was called here. It was called the Seven Years' War in Europe (1756–63).

The Spanish were, of course, already well established on this continent by the early 1500s. Hernando de Soto had been made governor of Florida by the king of Spain in 1538. By 1540, he and his army had already been into what is now Georgia. Eventually, they explored parts of what are now North and South Carolina, Tennessee and northern Alabama and Mississippi. In 1541, Soto and his army, which was now reduced to half its original size due to famine, disease, injury and warfare with the native inhabitants, discovered the Mississippi River. They named it Rio Grande. Whether any Spaniard ever made it up to the mouth of the Ohio River is not known. It was never recorded or documented if they did, but back then the Mississippi and the Ohio may have looked like parts of the same river, so they may have made it to that junction but had no reason to document it.

Written history tells us that by the mid-1600s, both France and England were aware that there was a great river that flowed westward. This they learned from the Native Americans, who spoke of such a river that flowed "to the great lake of salt water." But these Europeans, in their haste and excitement to discover a quicker route to the Orient, assumed that the natives were referring to the Pacific Ocean as the great lake of salt, when, of course, they were referring to the Gulf of Mexico and the Atlantic Ocean. The river didn't continue its westward course.

Historically, the credit for the discovery of the Ohio River has always gone to Frenchman René-Robert Cavelier, Sieur de La Salle, during the winter of 1669–70. Determined to find a short route to the Far East, he may or may not have traveled the Ohio. If he did, he did not claim it as such. But in 1671, the French laid formal claim to the American Northwest, so they most certainly were well aware of the river by that time.

Around the same time, the British were also aware that such a river existed. A British trapper and fur trader named Abraham Woods was trapping in the Ohio Valley in the mid-1600s, but like Cavelier, he did not formally claim it. It is safe to say that both French and English traders, explorers, trappers and hunters knew of the Ohio River at about the same time. So by 1700, the Ohio River, *La Belle Rivière* of the French, was fairly well known in its lower reaches, below the mouth of the Great Miami River, which is just upriver from Rabbit Hash on the opposite bank (right above the present I-275 bridge into Lawrenceburg).

In the second quarter of the eighteenth century, there were three major French expeditions down the Ohio River, each ten years apart. In 1729, a French engineer by the name of M. Chaussegros de Lery headed an expedition down the Ohio in which he made and recorded compass surveys of the river. His work later appeared in a map published in 1744 by a French cartographer, N. Bellin. Lery's expedition was accompanied and protected by a military entourage led by the French Canadian soldier and explorer Captain Charles Lemoyne de Longueil, the commander of Fort Niagara. Ten years later, in 1739, another expedition down the Ohio was led again by Longueil, this time to stop the hostile activities of the Chickasaws on the lower Mississippi. France was prepared to occupy the Ohio Valley. The steady intrusion of the French alarmed the English, especially the subjects living in Virginia and Maryland. So, the king of England ordered that 500,000 acres lying to the north of the Ohio between the mouth of the Kanawha and present-day Petersburg be granted to the Ohio Land Company of Virginia, to be settled by English families, in order to stop further French advancement. Then, in 1749, in response to this, the third major French military expedition took place.

Led by Pierre Joseph Celoron de Bienville, a French army ceremoniously marched down the Ohio River and periodically made proclamations of ownership for France. It was Celoron who buried those famed lead plates along the way, which in his mind settled once and for all any and all disputes of ownership. Celoron descended the Ohio all the way down to the mouth of the Great Miami River on the right bank (just above Lawrenceburg, Indiana, and across from Garrison Creek in Boone County) and then traveled its course as far as he could by water and then on foot. He visited various Indian settlements along the way. His mission of convincing the

Indians of the legitimacy of France's claims to the land and to persuade them to trade solely with French traders fell on deaf ears. For one thing, the natives could not comprehend the concept of anyone owning the Ohio River and its tributaries. Secondly, they were apparently satisfied with the trade arrangements and the treatment they had received in the past from the British traders and saw no benefit in dealing with the French. Celoron wrote, "All I can say is, that the tribes of these localities are very badly disposed toward the French and entirely devoted to the English."

The important thing here is that during the entire prehistoric era through the times of European contact, there was a lot of activity going on up and down the Ohio River in the vicinity of Rabbit Hash, Kentucky, especially between the mouth of the Great Miami River and the Big Bone Creek. But there was no town of Rabbit Hash—yet.

It would take another full one hundred years of bickering and wars between England and France, England and the various Native American cultures, England and the English colonists, the United States and England and then the United States and the Native American tribes before the Rabbit Hash General Store came into existence in 1831. It has been there ever since. It has served as the community clearinghouse for nine consecutive generations, if one accepts Thomas Jefferson's parameters for a generation as occurring every nineteen years. The general store has functioned just as the central plazas did for the prehistoric Fort Ancient people, as the council houses did for the Shawnee Indians or as the frontier forts did for the first frontiersmen and settlers of Kentucky. Humans have a basic need for socialization. Every society has either an established, designated meeting place or a commonly accepted informal gathering spot that serves as a sort of neutral zone for the society or community where information is gathered and exchanged, where community events and business are shared, where people intermingle with others who are not members of the core family unit and where ideas are discussed and problems solved. In Rabbit Hash, this place is the general store. This is where to place the point of the compass in order for the pencil to encircle and define the community.

2
WHY BUILD A TOWN ON THE BANKS OF A RIVER?

The Ohio River served as a major settlement route for post-glacier North America from the prehistoric era well into the nineteenth century—that is, almost twelve thousand years! The reason, of course, is obvious. The river provided all the necessities for subsistence of life and a simple, dependable medium for travel and trade. Due to these conveniences, the Native Americans built their towns and villages on its banks, and the Euro-Americans followed suit. Trial by error educated the inhabitants about floods and ice, and they adapted their choices for settlement locations accordingly, but still within proximity to the flowing waters. Every hundred years or so, the river painfully reminded the humans who was here first and who was the major force to be reckoned with on the continent. And eventually it sunk in, no pun intended.

There were three major Ohio River navigational landmarks that were known to all river travelers from the prehistoric era on into modern times. These are Split Rock (Ohio River Mile #500); Big Bone Lick, about two miles from the mouth of Big Bone Creek (Mile #514.6); and the Falls of the Ohio (Mile #601.6-604.5). In Boone County, Rabbit Hash was located right in the middle of two of these, Split Rock and Big Bone Lick. Right above Split Rock was a natural river crossing for the prehistoric megafauna and the bison herds that followed throughout historic times. And they made a trail from there to Big Bone Lick, one that eventually was utilized by other animals and humans alike. Portions of this trail made the foundation for roads and paths still used today.

On June 1, 1792, Kentucky became the fifteenth state. Boone County was formed in 1798 out of Campbell County on December 13 and slated to begin officially as a separate county "in June next," which would have been June 17, 1799, when the first county court of the Commission of Justices of the Peace officially met. The earliest established settlement in this stretch of the river was that of Tanner's Station (now Petersburg at mile 493.0) by the Reverend John Tanner in 1789. It is about eleven miles upriver from Rabbit Hash (mile 504.0). Tanner's Station was built on the site of two separate prehistoric Fort Ancient villages. This particular town site has never been affected by Ohio River flooding, which gives credence to the fact that the settlers paid particularly close attention to the habits and whims of the Ohio.

The early settlers in the Rabbit Hash and East Bend area (appropriately named for the corresponding meanders of the Ohio beginning around mile number 507.1) established their first homes along the river bottoms and the mouths of the creeks emptying into the river. There they found fertile farmland, food and water resources, as well as proximity to the transportation and trade resource, just like the native prehistoric and historic inhabitants had done. However, we find in many family histories and journals that these families soon moved the "home place" inland and upland onto the ridges. The reason most cited was to escape "the fever" or "ague." In the moist, humid swampy bottoms, the mosquito, with its disease-spreading capabilities, took its toll on the inhabitants.

About the same time that Boone County, Kentucky, was being established as Kentucky's thirtieth county (out of an eventual total of 120), similar activities were taking place across the river in what was considered the Indiana Territory, which was established out of the Northwest Territory in 1800 by the United States Congress. According to the *History of Dearborn and Ohio Counties, Indiana*, by 1814, two years before Indiana was to become a state, Rising Sun, Indiana Territory, had been laid out by John James. James was a planter from Frederick County, Maryland, who came to this area in 1807 by flatboat from Red Stone (Maysville) to Lawrenceburg, where he remained for two years before repairing upriver to Cincinnati, Ohio, for two more years. In 1811, he moved his family to Rising Sun, where they were sure to have witnessed the first steamboat (the *New Orleans*, built by Nicholas Roosevelt) to ply the Ohio River, both upstream and downstream, on its own power in October of that year, having passed the Rising Sun/Rabbit Hash area on two separate round trips to and from the Falls of the Ohio (Louisville, Kentucky).

There are several theories on the naming of the town of Rising Sun. One theory suggests that John James initially wanted to call it Jamestown in honor of the family surname, but being such an ardent admirer of nature, he found much pleasure in observing the rising sun each morning over the Kentucky hills across the river. He eventually decided on the name Rising Sun.

In 1816, Indiana was admitted to the Union as the nineteenth state. It was incorporated on September 1, 1817. About this same time, before the state was even one year old, Colonel A.C. Pepper traveled to Corydon, the state capital, to lobby for an act by the Indiana legislature organizing a new county, with Rising Sun as its seat of justice. However, he was unsuccessful.

Twenty-six miles below Cincinnati, Ohio, and four miles below Lawrenceburg, Indiana, Jessie Holman laid out the town of Aurora in 1819. Traveling downriver by boat, this new town was encountered just before the town of Rising Sun. Again, in nature, what precedes the rising sun each day in the horizon is an aurora, a brightening in the sky above the horizon just before the sun comes up. So the town that preceded Rising Sun came to be known as Aurora.

The history of the towns and settlement patterns across the river has a lot to do with the history of Rabbit Hash, Kentucky. The main channel of the Ohio River was along the Indiana side, and extensive sand bars littered the shoreline of the Kentucky side. Therefore, the newly established steamboat trade necessarily landed on the Indiana side of the river, due to the extremely shallow shore on the Kentucky side. In order for the people in the Rabbit Hash area to get their products up or downstream to market, they had to ferry them over to the Indiana side. Conversely, in order to receive items from up or downriver, they had to ferry over to Rising Sun to claim them and then ferry them back over.

Distance-wise, Rabbit Hash is closer to the town of Rising Sun than is the town's own western border. Early on, the people of both towns interacted and mingled. In low-water times, it was just like crossing the street to get to Rising Sun, only muddier. Throughout the towns' early histories, the people of Rabbit Hash attended church and school in Rising Sun, went to the doctor's in Rising Sun and courted, married and were buried in Rising Sun. Similarly, but not to the same extent, Rising Sun folks came to Rabbit Hash for certain services and goods, to visit family and friends and to purchase goods and products off the farms. Some corn products were more easily transported when reduced to fit into a Mason jar.

In the seasons when the river level was too high to wade across, ferryboats made the trips across just as simple and convenient, requiring, however, a small fee for the service. The Rabbit Hash Historical Society has in its collection, several of the ferry books kept by James Alexander Wilson, who not only operated the very first regular ferryboat between Rabbit Hash and Rising Sun but was also the first proprietor of the Rabbit Hash General Store (more on him in a later chapter).

Why did the ferry cross the river? So that two communities could be like one. This remained true for well over one hundred years. The residents of both towns interacted regularly on a daily basis until the ice of 1945 destroyed the last ferry communicating between the two locations. The icing on the cake was in the 1960s, with the completion of the current modern locks-and-dams system intended to ensure year-round river navigation. This major milestone project by the Army Corps of Engineers necessarily raised significantly the river levels throughout the entire 981-mile course of the Ohio but at the same time negatively impacted river communities like Rabbit Hash and Rising Sun along its banks.

Contrary to what the general public believes, this system of locks and dams has nothing at all to do with flood control. Their only purpose is to maintain year-round navigational pools for river commerce. There are flood-control measures built along the Ohio, but these are in the forms of preplanned flooding plains and retention areas.

Floods are basically what are responsible for the paucity of written and photographic primary documentary history of Rabbit Hash. Conversely, the lack of such devastating flooding damage to Rising Sun accounts for the more complete written record of that town's history. So a lot about Rabbit Hash is learned from the extant written history and newspaper accounts from across the river.

3

TRANSITION OF A GRANGE-BUILT STORAGE BUILDING INTO A GENERAL STORE

As more and more steamboats were making their way up and down the river and stopping regularly in Rising Sun, there was more and more communication back and forth across the river by way of ferryboat transport. People on the Kentucky side could now send across larger quantities of farm produce, grain and livestock destined for downriver markets. As more goods and services became available in Rising Sun, there was increased daily pedestrian and horse-powered-conveyance traffic on the ferry. Wagons, carts, carriages and buggies crossed the river just as easily as they could cross the street. Rabbit Hash folks regularly frequented Rising Sun for all their needs. They shopped, traded, conducted daily business, went to school and church, doctored, bought insurance and were even laid out and buried in Rising Sun. Some people even moved there and used the ferry to visit friends and family back in Rabbit Hash.

Sometime in 1830, several of the local Rabbit Hash farmers got together in one of their local Grange meetings and discussed joining forces and building a storehouse in Rabbit Hash near the ferryboat landing. Here they could bring their crops and produce and store them until it was time to ferry them across the river to load onto a steamboat. The Grange was another one of those social groups or clubs organized by like individuals with like interests and beliefs. It was an agrarian or agricultural-based organization. The whole idea of the Grange was Thomas Jefferson's when he recognized a social need for such an organization to be formed back in colonial times in Old Dominion, Virginia. Thomas Jefferson's vision for the new country, of

A postcard entitled "Birdseye View, Rising Sun, Ind." showing the peaceful river town of Rising Sun with Rabbit Hash in the background. The card is by the Kraemer Art Co., Cincinnati and Berlin, for distribution by William Green Jr., Rising Sun, Indiana (the postcard is unused and undated). *From the author's personal collection.*

course, was one of agrarian life composed of farmers and yeoman. Naturally, they would need a social organization with which to be associated that would offer guidance, instruction, cooperation and fellowship.

So the Rabbit Hash farmers cooperatively built a substantial, sturdy building for the purpose of storing goods waiting for transport up or downriver. The building they constructed was a thirty- by thirty-foot timber-framed bay with a gable roof of wooden shakes. It consisted of a joined rectangular-framed base of sill logs. At each corner was a mortise and tenon upright squared post, and these were mortised into a similar rectangular frame of plate logs. All the joints were pegged with wooden pegs. The resultant framed structure was built on solid rock foundation piers. Mortised and tenoned diagonal crosspieces were installed in each corner, up and down. There was no other wall framework. The walls were simply full two-inch-thick vertical random-width boards nailed to the plate logs on top and the sill logs on the bottom. A central doorway was placed in the front and the back, flanked by small windows on each side. This type of architecture is now described and identified as the Kentucky Boxed House.

As with any co-op, members took turns manning this storage facility and seeing to the loading and unloading of the crops and produce at specified times. Not long into the life of this co-op arrangement, it became apparent that if a member's time to mind the store were on a sunny, pleasant day, then the building would be left unattended, with the goods inside the building never making it to the steamboat on the opposite shore. It seems the farmer member in charge would deem a sunny day more conducive to cutting, putting up hay or some similarly related farming chore, so he would abandon the store in favor of getting his crops in.

This is where seventeen-year-old James Alexander Wilson entered the picture. In 1831, he was to become the very first proprietor of the Rabbit Hash General Store, although at the time it was probably just referred to as "the storehouse," "the store" or "Wilson's store." He also assisted in the operation of the ferry between this place and Rising Sun, Indiana. James A., as his descendants referred to him, was born in Culpepper Court House, Madison County, Virginia, on November 17, 1814. At the age of ten, his parents moved the family to Boone County, Kentucky, and settled near Petersburg. Two years later, in 1826, they moved downriver to Rabbit Hash, where James A. spent the remainder of his life.

Along about 1837, he also served as the Boone County constable for the magisterial precinct of Carlton, which happened to be what the area was

Professional portrait photograph of James A. Wilson, the very first proprietor of the general store in Rabbit Hash, Kentucky. *From the Rabbit Hash Historical Society collection.*

called prior to its more famous and popular name of Rabbit Hash. The Rabbit Hash Historical Society has in its possession two of James A. Wilson's Constable Day Books, which together were a running written account of the duties performed by him as constable. His handwritten index perhaps best explains the duties of a county constable:

Index to Constables Book	*Page*
Warrants for Debt	*1*
Levying Executions	*2*
*Replevin Bonds**	3
Forthcoming Bonds	*4*
Commission	*5*
Summoning Witness	*6*
Constable Day Book	*19-20-21-22-23-24*
Leg-Attachments	*Page 7*

*According to *Webster's Universal Dictionary of the English Language* (1937), *replevin* is "1) In law, an action for the recovery of personal property unlawfully detained; 2) The writ or process by which property is replevied."

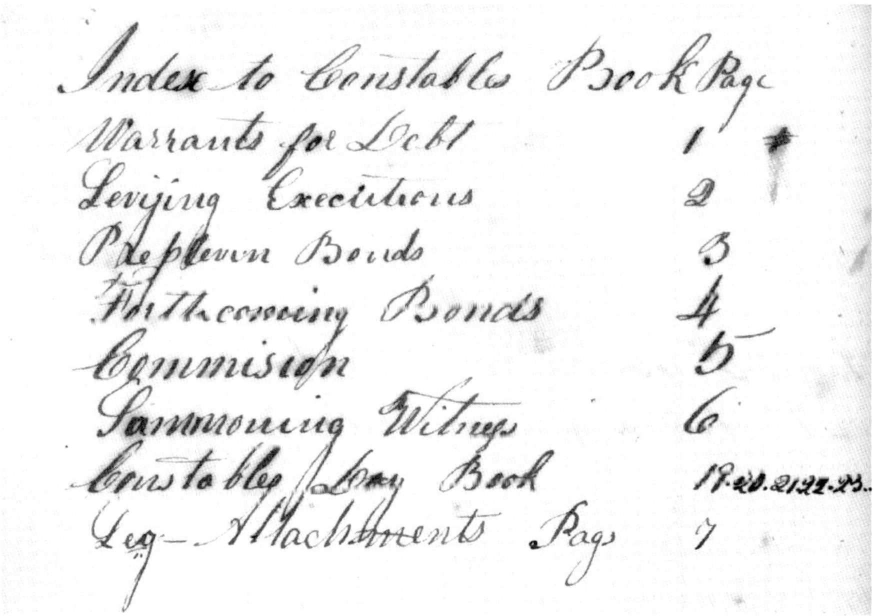
Index to Constables Book Page
Warrants for Debt 1
Levying Executions 2
Replevin Bonds 3
Forthcoming Bonds 4
Commision 5
Summoning Witnes 6
Constables Day Book 19.20.21.22.23..
Leg-Attachments Page 7

The index page to James A. Wilson's Constable's Day Book. *From the Rabbit Hash Historical Society collection.*

On June 5, 1837, he recorded:

> *Received of Mr. Wm. Kirtley for Safe Keeping and collection a note of hand against Randolph Rice and in favor of Walter Hunt assigned to Milton Kirtley to the amount of forty-four dollars. Dew May 21st. J.A.W. C.B.C.*

Then, on September 23, 1837, he noted in his book:

> *Sold as the Property of Randolph Rice 65¼ cords of wood to Milton Kirtley at Public Constables Sale at 15 cts per cord which satisfies in full an execution against Sd.* [said] *Rice and in favor of Milton Kirtley the amount 48 dollars 97½ Cts, J.A. Wilson C.B.C.*

The following information comes from his obituary, printed in a local newspaper:

A family photograph of patriarch James Alexander and his wife, Jane Kendall (Stephens) Wilson, with eight of their thirteen children, four of whom did not survive childhood and one of whom, John M. Wilson, was killed at Perryville, Kentucky, during the Civil War. *From left to right, top row (standing)*: Samuel C., Robert M., Charles, Thomas A. and George H. *Bottom row (seated)*: Mary Lou (Wilson) Craig, Quintus N., Jane K., James A. and Benjamin. *From the Rabbit Hash Historical Society collection.*

Robert Haydon Wilson in the Wilson family graveyard, by Karl Kuntz, 1980. Wilson always said that he wanted to be buried in the "family plot at the old home place," next to his father and grandfather, but his wish was not realized. He was interred at the East Bend Methodist Church Cemetery in May 1986. *From the Rabbit Hash Historical Society collection.*

> *On October 2, 1842, he married Jane K. Stephens. Together they had thirteen children. About this time, he took charge over the operation of the Rabbit Hash–Rising Sun ferry, which he operated for about almost seven years. He was twice elected a member of the Kentucky legislature, from 1866 to 1868 and from 1873 to 1874, where he served with honor to himself and credit to his constituency. He served his county as school commissioner and was for many years deputy county clerk, as well as county constable. He died on September 16, 1904, at the age of 89 years, 10 months and 29 days. He was interred in the Wilson Family Cemetery on his old home place property, where he lived with his wife and children since 1850.*

James A. continued to operate the ferry until 1849, when James Carlton and James Calvert took over the operation. Wilson continued running the store. Just as he kept records in his Constable Day Book, he also kept an accurate daily ferryboat ledger. The Rabbit Hash Historical Society also has possession of one of his ferry ledgers, which runs from October 3, 1846, to April 25, 1849. He called the book the "Rising Sun Ferry," and in it he recorded

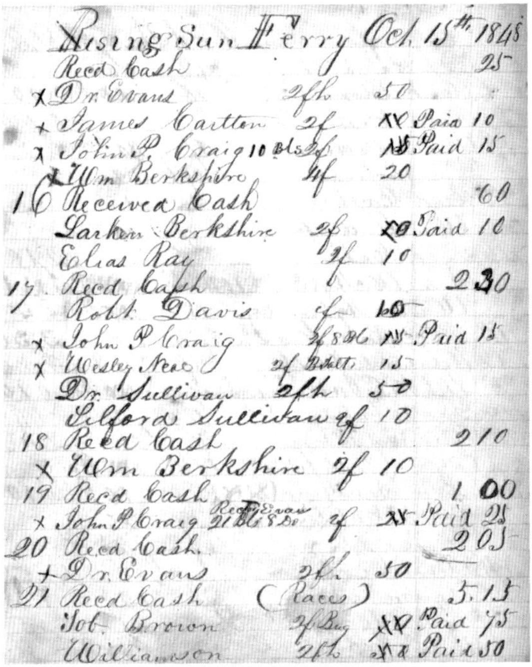

Rising Sun Ferry Oct 15th 1848
Recd Cash 25
x Dr Evans 2fh 50
x James Carlton 2f XX Paid 10
x John P Craig 10 Bls 2f XX Paid 15
x Wm Berkshire 4f 20
16 Received Cash 60
Larkin Berkshire 2f XX Paid 10
Elias Ray 2f 10
17 Recd Cash 2 30
Robt Davis f 10
x John P Craig 2f 8 Bls XX Paid 15
x Wesley Neal 2f 2 Bls 15
Dr Sullivan 2fh 50
Silford Sullivan 2f 10
18 Recd Cash 2 10
x Wm Berkshire 2f 10
19 Recd Cash 1 00
x John P Craig 21 Bls 2f XX Paid 25
20 Recd Cash 2 05
+ Dr Evans 2fh 50
21 Recd Cash (Races) 5.15
Jol Brown 2f Bug XX Paid 75
Williamson 2fh XX Paid 50

A page from James A. Wilson's Rising Sun Ferry book dated October 15, 1848, showing the receipts of the day and subsequent days, as well as the names of passengers. *From the Rabbit Hash Historical Society collection.*

the date, the person's name, the fee, whether the fee was collected and, at the end of each day, the total amount collected. Sometimes he recorded what goods the passenger was hauling and sometimes the weather and the river conditions. From November 23, 1847, through December 17, he noted when it rained and when the river was running high. (This was during the 1847 flood, which will be discussed in a later chapter.) Wilson was even running the ferry on Christmas Day that year.

The surviving Ferry Keeper's Bonds and Court Order Books at Boone County Courthouse in Burlington, Kentucky, provide a fairly accurate record of the subsequent Rising Sun Ferry owners. Luckily, these bonds are extant in the Boone County Courthouse; since the official boundary of Kentucky was always the low-water mark on the opposite shore, the Ohio River was always under the legal jurisdiction of Kentucky, and consequently, all the ferry keeper's bonds and licenses were the responsibility of Kentucky counties.

RISING SUN FERRY OWNERS AND YEAR OF OPERATION AND OWNERSHIP

1849 James Carlton and James Calvert
1852 John Quincy Adams Stephens
1855 Pembroke Ryle
1856 Thaddeus Constantine Sobieski Ryle and William Rice
1858 William P. Ryle

1859 Leonard Clore (this is the earliest date that mentions the town name of Rabbit Hash)
1861 James Calvert
1867 James Perkins
1872 Robert Piatt
1874 Richard S. Ryle
1875 Robert Piatt
1888 John J. Huey
1890 Thomas Lumpkins
1899 Benjamin Wilson (son of James A.)
1899 Josie R. Piatt, Katie Piatt Bottorf and C.M. Bottorf, Susie Piatt Greenup and George H. Greenup
1906 Benjamin Wilson

Since 1906, no other ferry keeper's bonds have been located in the Boone County Courthouse, but in the possession of the Rabbit Hash Historical

J.W. Whitlock and his famous Hoosier Boy. *From the Rabbit Hash Historical Society collection (donated by Wanetta Clause).*

Society is a handwritten note, dated 1981, by William J. "Bill" Stephens. He was in his nineties at the time and was asked to write down some of his memoirs for the historical society. His grammar and spelling weren't the best, but his memory was. He reported that for as long as he could remember, the ferry was operated by Ben Wilson but owned by Josie Piatt. She lived in Rising Sun and eventually sold the ferry franchise to J.W.Whitlock of Rising Sun. Whitlock was a local furniture factory owner whose passion and hobby was building boats. He is famous for building the Hoosier Boy and the Hoosier Girl, which were early hydroplane racing boats. Whitlock still to this day holds the world hydroplane speed record, traveling from Cincinnati, Ohio, to Louisville, Kentucky, and back at a mile a minute. He made this record run in high water when all the dams were covered. The record has never been broken because of the newer high-water dams that replaced the old wooden wicket dams, necessitating that newer boats lock through on both the downriver trip and then again upriver.

Stephens said that Clarence "Windy" Bedgood and Ben Harris both operated the ferry for Whitlock for many years. Then, Raymond Bedgood, Windy's bachelor brother, took over until "the ice finally got her [the ferry]." This was in 1945.

The *Rising Sun and Ohio County Sesquicentennial* booklet from 1964 concurs that the last ferryboat to operate between Rising Sun, Indiana, and Rabbit Hash, Kentucky, was indeed the *Mildred*, which was built in 1922 by Whitlock. Operators of the *Mildred*, at various times, included Ben Harris, Frank Cunningham, Clarence Bedgood, Stewart Whitlock and, finally, Raymond

Two of the old-timers and premier history chroniclers from the era of the resurrection of the town of Rabbit Hash in the late 1970s. Robert Haydon Wilson is seated on the right, holding his dog, and "old" Bill Stephens is on the left. The old Rabbit Hash Post Office pigeonholes for mail can be seen in the upper left background. *From the Rabbit Hash Historical Society collection.*

Bedgood, who took over the business from Whitlock in 1937 until 1945, when he quit the business, dismantled the boat and sold the hull to a boat club in Carrollton, Kentucky. Unfortunately, the hull sank and eventually washed ashore at Rising Sun before it ever made it to Carrollton. This ended the more than one-hundred-year regular ferryboat service between the two towns forever. Ice and floods were the eternal demons of Mother Nature that preyed on the little town of Rabbit Hash, Kentucky.

The *Mildred* was designed and built by J.W. Whitlock of Rising Sun, the famous racing boat builder in the early 1900s. It would be the very last car ferry between Rabbit Hash and Rising Sun, meeting its final demise in the ice of the winter of 1944–45. It belonged to Raymond Bedgood at the time; he had planned to sell the hull for reuse, but the boat sank before that could occur. *From the Rabbit Hash Historical Society collection.*

When the local farmers of the Grange first agreed to jointly build and operate that very first storehouse on the Boone County banks of the Ohio River, little did they know they were constructing an endearing reminder of their cultural history. The structure was more than just a shed for produce storage. It was the beginning of a community that would house less tangible and more abstract things than tobacco, hay and grains. It harbored determination, aspiration, care, concern, friendship, growth, unity, purpose and cooperation. It served as a church, school and community center. It represented equality, fairness, honesty and morality. It was the heartbeat and soul of their community. Throughout every generation, it continued to function in these capacities. Still, to this day, the store is the centerpiece of the community and town. That is, and will remain, its legacy.

Unlike the Rabbit Hash Ferry business, which seemed to change owners and operators fairly regularly, the opposite held true for the general store. From 1831 until 1919, it remained in the Wilson family. The exact date is not known, but James A. took in a partner by the name of Cal Riddell. This was the situation in 1894, when Reuben Gold Thwaites visited Rabbit Hash on his historic travel adventure from Pittsburgh to New Orleans and took the photograph of the Wilson and Riddell store on the cover of this book. When James A. died in 1904, his son Ben inherited the property and business, keeping Cal Riddell to operate it. Calvin Garnet Riddle (February 14, 1851–November 19, 1921) actually lived with Ben Wilson and his wife. In his obituary, it was recorded that he

> *was born and reared on the farm, and attended the common schools of the county, and after reaching manhood taught in the public schools for several years. In 1877 he became a clerk in the Granger store at Rabbit Hash; in 1883 the business became the property of Wilson & Riddle; in the spring of 1900 Mr. Wilson's interest was sold to L.L. Stephens, which business was carried on under the firm name of Riddle and Stephens and the store was run under that name for three years, when Mr. Riddle bought out his partner, and which he owned at the time of his death.*

Even though James A. sold his part of the business to Stephens, the building and property itself remained in the Wilson family. His son Ben was running the Rising Sun/Rabbit Hash Ferry at the time he inherited the store property and had no share in the partnership of the general store business itself. The article goes on to further state that Cal was laid out in the home of Mrs. Ben Wilson (Ben Wilson had just died about a month earlier, on October 16, 1921) after being properly prepared by undertaker C. Scott Chambers:

> *"Cal" as he was called, was praised for his many good qualities…He was never married. He leaves several nephews and nieces…Rev. R.C. McNeely conducted a short funeral service in the K. of P. Hall in Rabbit Hash, which was filled, as was the yard surrounding the hall. A quartette from Rising Sun rendered several beautiful and appropriate songs.*
>
> *Funeral service was conducted by the Masonic and K. of P. orders of which he had been a member for a number of years. After the service his remains were brought to Burlington and buried on the lot with his father and mother, sister and brother, there to rest until resurrection day.*

Cal Riddell standing on the front porch of the Wilson and Riddell general store in the last decade of the nineteenth century. *From the Rabbit Hash Historical Society collection.*

Cal Riddell with his mules and wagon pulled up to a side bay of the Rabbit Hash General Store, circa 1894. *Courtesy of the Rabbit Hash Historical Society.*

Left: An "In Memoriam" pin-back ribbon badge from East Bend Lodge No. 114 Knights of Pythias Lodge of Rabbit Hash, Kentucky. During the funeral services for Cal Riddell and Benjamin Wilson held in the Rabbit Hash Knights of Pythias Hall, this badge would have been prominently displayed on the body, as well as worn by the other members. *From the Rabbit Hash Historical Society collection.*

Opposite top: A "Rec'd Payment in full" receipt to Charles W. Craig from "C.G. Riddell, Dealer in General Merchandise" dated "Rabbit Hash, Ky., Mar 2, 1912." Note the statement, "Country Produce Taken in Exchange for Goods." This had always been the case in Rabbit Hash and continued to be into the future of the general store. The folded envelope is from after 1919, when the same C.W. Craig took ownership of the store and business. *From the Rabbit Hash Historical Society collection (donated by Lib Stephens).*

Opposite bottom: A "C.W. Craig General Mdse." souvenir postcard. Since 1919, there has always been a Coca-Cola sign on the front of the store. *From the author's personal collection*

In 1919, C.W. Craig purchased the store, and the name changed to C.W. Craig's General Store. When he died in 1945, his wife, Emma, inherited the store and business, and their son, William Jennings Craig, took over the business. It remained in the hands of the Craig family until Louie Scott purchased it in 1978 from another Craig sibling. Approximately 147 years of continuous operation under the ownership of basically two separate families is quite a feat in the mom-and-pop business world! Louie retained sole ownership of the store (and the whole town) until 2002, when he sold it lock, stock and barrel to the Rabbit Hash Historical Society.

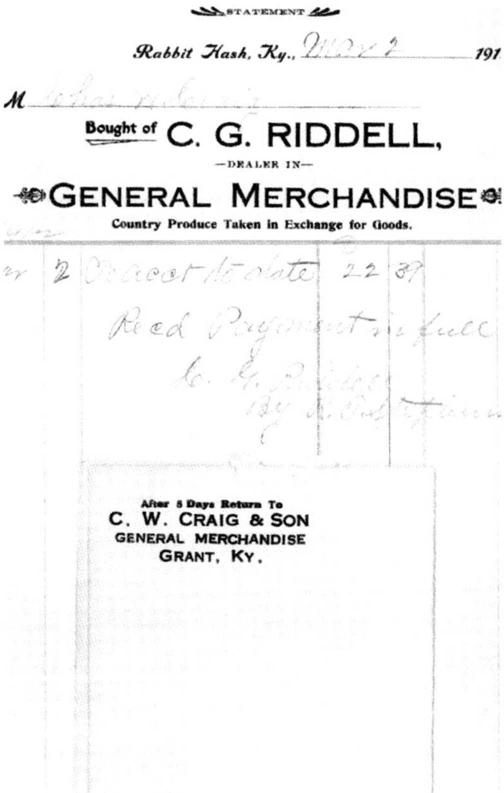
STATEMENT

Rabbit Hash, Ky., ______ 191

M ______

Bought of C. G. RIDDELL,

—DEALER IN—

GENERAL MERCHANDISE

Country Produce Taken in Exchange for Goods.

2 Acct to date 22 39

Recd Payment in full

After 5 Days Return To
C. W. CRAIG & SON
GENERAL MERCHANDISE
GRANT, KY.

4
A COMMUNITY VERSUS MOTHER NATURE'S FORCES

Threatened by Floods and Ice

Back when our ancestors settled this North American continent, the Ohio River played an important role in settlement patterns, sustenance and subsistence. It just made good sense to settle and establish one's home and community on the banks of the very river that supplied a food and water source, as well as a convenient mode of travel and locomotion, which in turn provided for trade, commerce and a certain primitive economy. The river was the settlers' friend, companion, protector and sense of stability.

The settlers knew the river could turn on them at any time. But they chose to play the law of averages as opposed to move away from such a necessary resource. They had no weathermen or means of forecasting what nature was going to throw their way. It was a crapshoot, and sometimes they got caught in the crap.

Ohio River floods historically have wreaked havoc on the small river hamlet of Rabbit Hash. The first one of major significance was the 1847 flood, which reached a depth of 67.6 feet. This late November/early December inundation was the result of extraordinary rainfall throughout the month of November. According to National Register Service statistics, the sixty-five-plus inches of rain during the year had been the record rainfall in the area until 2011 (over 164 years), when the total topped the sixty-seven-inch mark.

Minor flooding occurs regularly, usually in the spring or fall, but it can happen anytime when the conditions are just right. There have been some fairly significant summer floods. The next major Rabbit Hash flooding occurred in the back-to-back years of 1883 (68.0 feet) and 1884 (71.1 feet), each surpassing the mark set in 1847. There is an old axiom that people living along the river respect and live by: the Ohio River will always come back for what it left behind in previous attacks. This has proven to be true many more times than not. To demonstrate just how much the people of Rabbit Hash believe this, take the general store as an example. After the inundations of 1883, the townspeople took proactive measures to ensure the safety of the general store. They devised a system of inch-diameter iron stock rods bored through the top plate logs and down through the sill logs of the structure with blacksmith-made hooks on the ends. A similar set of bars with hand-forged hooks is permanently anchored in the ground, lining up hook to hook with the others. When the water gets under the store and begins to float it, the hooks engage and securely hold the building in place. This proved to be quite foresighted because the 1884 flood and the 1913 flood both reached 71.0 feet, only to be undercut by the 1907 rendition at 65.2 feet and two floods in 1913. One in January crested at 62.2 feet, and the second flood later in April topped the 70-foot mark.

A series of blacksmith-made hand-forged rods with hooks fashioned on the ends runs vertically through the sill logs and the plate logs of the framework of the general store. Similar rods with hooks are secured to the ground in concrete beneath each one that is bored through the building. When floodwaters get high enough to float the building, these hooks engage and hold the building securely in place. *Photograph by the author.*

Four adventurous young ladies surveyed the flood of 1948 in a johnboat in front of the general store. *From the Rabbit Hash Historical Society collection.*

The Rabbit Hash General Store in the flood of 1997 is securely anchored and not going anywhere, just as it was in 1964, 1948, 1937, 1933 and 1913. *From the Rabbit Hash Historical Society collection.*

Most people believed that a higher water level than that in 1907 or 1913 wasn't possible. The people in Rabbit Hash just *hoped* that there never would be higher water. But they knew the wrath of the old gal. The year 1918 greeted them with a solidly frozen river that ultimately sent destructive ice floes downriver, resulting in a flood with a crest of 61.8 feet in February. The year 1933 offered a river level of 63.6 feet in March. When the 1937 flood crested at 82.5 feet in Lawrenceburg, Indiana, a few miles upriver, half the town of Rabbit Hash was swept away. The official reading at Cincinnati was 79.9 feet. It had always been said that this 79.9-foot level was declared the official reading because most of the insurance policies on property on or near the river in Cincinnati carried rider clauses that declared the policy null and void if the river ever reached 80.0 feet, but to this day that belief has never been documented in the literature.

The 1937 flood was the mother of all floods. Its destruction and ruination of lives, careers, businesses, fortunes, economy, trade and commerce, homes, schools, churches, communities and every aspect of second-quarter twentieth-century humanity spared no one within its wicked, chilling grasp along all 981 miles of the Ohio and the 1,000-plus more miles of the lower

The ice of 1918 piled up on the Rising Sun shore as people posed for this photograph with Rabbit Hash in the background. *From the Rabbit Hash Historical Society collection.*

A "big" river passes by Dr. I.E. Carlisle's house, garden, outbuildings and road during the 1913 flood. *From the Rabbit Hash Historical Society collection.*

The high waters of the 1933 flood threatened homes in Rabbit Hash but did not wash them all away. The old river adage "The Ohio River will come back for whatever it left behind" proved so true just four years later when the 1937 flood literally took half the town. *From the Rabbit Hash Historical Society collection.*

Mississippi. It was by far the worst natural disaster ever to occur in the continental United States to date.

Thousands of people never returned to the Ohio's banks. The same was true in Rabbit Hash. But there were others who chose to try it again, hoping there would never be a repeat of this magnitude. The 1937 flood completely covered the Rabbit Hash General Store, except for the very peak of the roof. To this day, there is still river mud in the attic and on the roof rafters. Had it not been for those ingenious blacksmiths fifty years before, the store would be gone, and the saga of Rabbit Hash, Kentucky, would have ended there.

But quality of life choices, faith and determination resurrected this doomed little Ohio River village and gave it another chance. C.W. Craig, who had owned the store since 1919, continued operation until 1945. Even after his death, it remained in the family, owned by his wife, Emma Craig. Their son, William Jennings Craig, worked there as a store clerk and offered many other business services like general hauling, farming, livestock and anything else he could come up with to make money. He was even the county dogcatcher. He was always known by his nickname, "Sheeny

The *Mildred* lands right in front of the general store as the '37 floodwaters continue to advance. A truck loads onto the ferryboat for the trip across river to Rising Sun. *From the Rabbit Hash Historical Society collection.*

The huckster truck getting ready to evacuate the store buildings in town as the waters of the 1937 flood encroach on the lives and sustenance of the unsuspecting townsfolk. *From the Rabbit Hash Historical Society collection.*

Craig." Sheeny was a culturally derogatory term for a Jew, but he didn't mind the name at all. He knew it was just an endearing term that the locals had for him, and it may well have been. But they made sure they were on their toes when it came to dealing with him. (This is presented here only for the purpose of explaining a historic fact and is not intended to propagate an ethnic slur.) Sheeny's sister, Lib, and her husband, Cliff, also clerked in the store along with the rest of the family. Miss Emma, their mother, was generally there sweeping and clerking, but she left the business operation up to Sheeny. He remained there until June 15, 1967, when he was evicted by the Boone County sheriff. According to a local newspaper account dated Monday, June 26, 1967:

> *William Jennings (Sheeny) Craig, 61, was evicted at 2 p.m. Saturday from the general store he had operated in Rabbit Hash since 1919.* [It was actually owned and operated by his father, C.W. Craig. In 1919, Sheeny would only have been thirteen years old.] *"I hated to leave," Craig said. "But I simply turned over the keys to the sheriff after I had him take a look inside to see that everything was all right."*
>
> *Craig said he had previously moved everything from the building.*

Craig is Boone County dog warden as well as one of the oldest businessmen in the small Ohio River community.

At one time he wore the mantle of "Mayor" of Rabbit Hash. [Ironically, the past three contemporary mayors of Rabbit Hash have all been dogs, which undoubtedly would not have approved of Sheeny's elected county office.]

Craig said he lost title to the store property when he and his wife, Frances, were divorced.

"I had the store in her name and she took it with her when we separated. Then she sold it to Clifford Stephens." [Cliff was the husband of Sheeny's sister, Pearl Elizabeth (Lib) Craig Stephens.]

Stephens demanded his property around May 1 of this year. When Craig had not moved on June 15, Judge Bruce Ferguson ordered him to vacate the premises.

"I had no other choice than to let the sheriff throw me out," Craig said. His mother, Mrs. Emma Craig, 80, with whom Craig makes his home, was with him on the last walk out of the store.

"But I still answer to the store number, 586-6821," Craig said. "I have to have some place [rural party line] *that people can call me about dogs." Lib and Cliff continued to run the store up until 1979, at which time they sold out to Louie Scott.*

The same year that marked the death of Sheeny's father, C.W. Craig, and his last year (1945) at the store, destructive ice broke up the *Mildred*, the very last Rising Sun–Rabbit Hash ferryboat, and its encore was a 69.2-foot-crest March flood. The Craig family just pulled up their bootstraps and continued operations into the late 1960s. In 1948, they had to battle another store-clearing flood of 64.8 feet. By this time, there was no river commerce or economy whatsoever. The railroads and the improved highway systems, along with the highly dependable automobile, changed forever the trade and commerce of Rabbit Hash. No one depended on the river for transportation of farm products and goods. As a matter of fact, most of the younger generation left the farm completely and opted for city jobs. Groceries, hardware and clothing—and all the other "potions and notions"—were more conveniently obtained and sometimes less expensive in town. This was a national trend for every small river community. People finally turned their backs on the river. New navigational locks and dams raised the river level from sixteen to twenty-six feet in Rabbit Hash, covering precious farming bottomlands and other personal property. Some

Advertisement for the bus line that ran from Rabbit Hash to Covington and back. *From the Rabbit Hash Historical Society collection (donated by Lib Stephens).*

Rickey and Babe Stephens, along with Wendell, Cindy and John Ryle, checking out the floodwaters and the general store in the 1964 Ohio River flood. *From the Rabbit Hash Historical Society collection.*

small towns even lost entire streets and all the buildings that prior floods had spared. There would be no repeat of 1937; floodwalls would see to that, at least in the cities of more renown and importance. Rabbit Hash, however, would have to fend for itself.

Evacuating the general store—people load boxes of groceries and stock into a school bus during the 1964 high water. *From the Rabbit Hash Historical Society collection.*

Maybe the folks in Rabbit Hash were becoming too complacent after the 1948 ordeal. Just to remind them again who was boss, the Ohio blessed them with a teaser in 1955 at sixty-one feet, lapping the front porch but not getting into the general store. About sixty-two feet sends water into the store, and sixty-four feet gets it about waist high and up to the countertops.

Boom! On March 1964, 66.2 feet of water just about tried the patience of the storekeepers once and for all. Just as things were getting on an even keel, the river warned them once again. It was almost like the Rabbit Hash General Store was taunting, "Come and get me if you can."

Historically, whenever high waters threatened the town and the general store, the community went into action, almost as if it had been having fire drills on a regular basis. People knew the drill. They all gathered at the store with horses and wagons, completely emptied the store of all its contents and drove the wagons into a neighbor's barn up on the hill. Simple as that. They all knew when to show up and what to do when they got there. When the waters subsided, they cleaned out the mess, disinfected and dried out the building and then brought all of the stock back down. If somebody needed goods in the meantime, they could be purchased right off the wagon in the barn. The slabs of bologna and cheese were generally consumed during the move, so there was no worry about perishable food going to waste.

5
WHY RABBIT HASH?

A historian depends on recorded and documented facts and information. Primary resources are always the mother lode when writing the history of a small town. But what happens when a small town like Rabbit Hash is devastated time and time again by destructive floodwaters sweeping away books, records, letters, photographs, personal property and heirlooms and even the physical half of the town itself? With these kinds of losses, a historically accurate rendition of the place in question is, to say the least, tentative if not impossible. But all is not lost as long as there are old-timers around. The focus merely shifts from a purely historical approach to one of oral history and memoirs, or a folklorist approach.

How and why did this town get named Rabbit Hash? There have been several stories created and propagated over the years attempting to answer these questions. All of them, of course, have one common denominator: the fact that an abundance of rabbits provided a fairly dependable food staple called rabbit stew or hash.

One oft-repeated tale explains that steamboat travelers would ferry across the river from Rising Sun and inquire about what was being served at Meeks's Tavern. Of course, the answer was always rabbit hash. There was a Meeks's Landing and an Edward Meeks, who secured the very first ferry keepers' bond in Boone County in 1813. But the landing was located about three miles upriver from Rabbit Hash. Why would anyone traveling on a steamboat that had landed at Rising Sun want to cross the river to the Kentucky side in the first place? There was no commercial activity located there around this time.

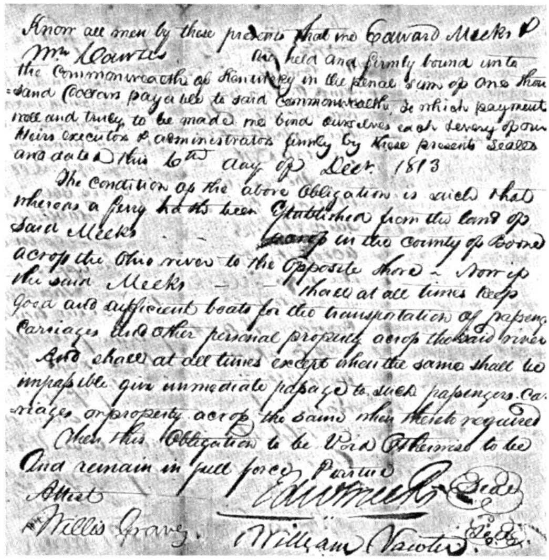

Know all men by these presents that we Edward Meeks &
Wm [illegible] are held and firmly bound unto
the Commonwealth of Kentucky in the penal sum of One thou
=sand Dollars payable to said Commonwealth, to which payment
well and truly to be made we bind ourselves each severally & our
heirs executors & administrators firmly by these presents sealed
and dated this 6th day of Decr 1813
The Condition of the above Obligation is such that
whereas a ferry hath been Established from the land of
said Meeks [illegible] in the County of Boone
across the Ohio river to the Opposite shore - Now if
the said Meeks - shall at all times keep
good and sufficient boats for the transportation of passeng
Carriages and other personal property across the said river
And shall at all times except when the same shall be
impassible give immediate passage to such passengers Car
=riages or property across the same when thereto required
then this Obligation to be Void Otherwise to be
And remain in full force
Attest Edward Meeks (Seal)
Willis Graves William [illegible] (Seal)

A copy of the ferry bond granted to Edward Meeks in 1813. It has long been the erroneous belief that Meeks's ferry was located at the future town site of Rabbit Hash. It was actually located about a mile upriver in present-day Belleview Bottoms, near the mouth of Middle Creek. It was still the first ferryboat crossing the river to where Rising Sun would soon be established the following year. This is the earliest ferry bond on record at the Boone County Courthouse. *From the author's personal collection.*

This particular story explained that salt agents who were headed to Big Bone Lick would cross at Rising Sun. Big Bone Lick was a well-known salt springs and gathering place for animals that had come to lick the salt-encrusted earth since all the way back in time to the Pleistocene era, dating about twelve thousand years ago. It had become the famous mastodon, mammoth and bison graveyard and bone-collection spot on the North American continent. It was renowned worldwide because of this resource of Pleistocene remains. However, this attribute could not account for a need for a ferry because the traffic would be almost nonexistent. The saline waters there were much more diluted than at other saltworks in Kentucky, so the yield of salt per hundreds of gallons of saline was too low for the place to have ever been a commercial salt manufactory. This myth has no supporting evidence.

Another story that circulated in the past—more so then than now—explained that the Shawnee captive Mary Ingles, while traveling with a band of her captors on a salt-making expedition to Big Bone Lick, stopped to camp one night exactly where Rabbit Hash is located, and she cooked up some rabbit hash for her captors' dinner. This is pure bunk. That Mary Ingles passed through as a Shawnee captive is true, but this occurred in 1755, long before any white man had ever settled in this area. There would be no local memory of this event to inspire such a name for the location.

What is considered and accepted as the real story of the naming of Rabbit Hash is found in a publication entitled *The Buried Treasure: A Rabbit Hash Mystery*, by William H. Nelson. The book has no date of publication,

William H. Nelson, author of *The Buried Treasure: A Rabbit Hash Mystery. From the Rabbit Hash Historical Society collection.*

but extant information on Nelson places the publication sometime in the 1890s. At the end of the booklet is a reprinted article entitled "Rabbit Hash, Kentucky: The Origin of Its Name," which was originally written for the *Lawrenceburg Register*. Some of what is known about William H. Nelson is that besides working as a blacksmith for a time in Rabbit Hash and as a schoolteacher, he also worked in some capacity with the Lawrenceburg newspaper. He was also associated with the Rising Sun newspaper, purportedly as editor.

The featured story of this publication, "The Buried Treasure," was based on an actual historic event. In the summer of 1781, General George Rogers Clark requested that Colonel Archibald Lochry, an American army officer from Pennsylvania, raise a militia and join the general in Wheeling, (West) Virginia, for a military campaign against the British in Detroit. Lochry had trouble raising the requested 300 men, and this delay caused him to miss his rendezvous with Clark. A message at Wheeling informed Lochry to proceed downriver to meet at the mouth of the Little Kanawha River, a rendezvous he also missed due to Clark's men deserting near the settlements there, forcing the general to move on downriver. Next, Lochry was to catch up with Clark at the mouth of the Great Miami River. He failed again. So Lochry sent a small group of men by boat, with a letter to the general, to catch up to Clark and his men. Lochry continued down with his force, which now numbered 106 men.

A couple days later, he came upon two of the men sent to catch Clark. They reported that they had been ambushed by Indians, who killed and scalped the others and confiscated the letter. Lochry then ordered his men to travel nonstop downriver. Several days later, hunger was overtaking his men when they spotted a deer at the mouth of a creek on the Indian side of the river (Indiana bank). They pulled in their boats, butchered the deer and started a cooking fire. Suddenly, they were ambushed by Indians hiding in the brush on the bank. They fired back and made for the middle of the river with the boats, only to be caught in crossfire from Indians hiding out on the Kentucky side. In the end, forty men were killed and scalped and sixty-four taken prisoner, including Colonel Lochry. While he was in Indian custody, Lochry was sitting on a log as the prisoners were being divided up amongst the several tribes. He was suddenly dispatched from behind by one of the Shawnee band by a tomahawk blow splitting his skull. He was then reportedly scalped while still alive and died shortly thereafter.

There is no record of those slain that day ever being removed or buried. It is hoped that the cleansing floodwaters of the Ohio River have laid those bones to rest. Over the years, the name of the creek that was the site of this horrific massacre that occurred in the final year of the American Revolution has metamorphosed from Lochry to Laughery (located at Ohio River Mile #496.6). There remains today an island in the middle of the stream just a little below the mouth of the creek known as Laughery Island (Ohio River Mile #499.2). (Ohio River miles are calculated as being the number of miles downstream from the source where the Allegheny River meets the Monongahela River at Pittsburgh). In 1924, the Lawrenceburg, Indiana chapter of the Daughters of the American Revolution erected a monument to mark the site of Lochry's defeat. The monument includes the names of those unfortunate men who lost their lives that day. It is located within the River View Cemetery on State Route 56, at Laughery Creek Road in Aurora, Indiana. Laughery Creek is the dividing line between Dearborn and Ohio Counties in southeastern Indiana.

It was at this point that William H. Nelson took up the story. His tale centered on two highly trusted members of Lochry's force whom, in the height of battle with the ambushing Indians, the colonel singled out to carry out what would be one of his last official orders as an army officer. They were to clandestinely leave the battle with a bag of Spanish gold coin, which was to be distributed among certain stations along the Kentucky side of the river. The two chosen men were remiss to leave the colonel and the rest of the men but took up their charge with confidence and speed and successfully made their way to the Kentucky shore unnoticed. They disappeared into the surrounding Kentucky hills with the treasure, never losing sight of the

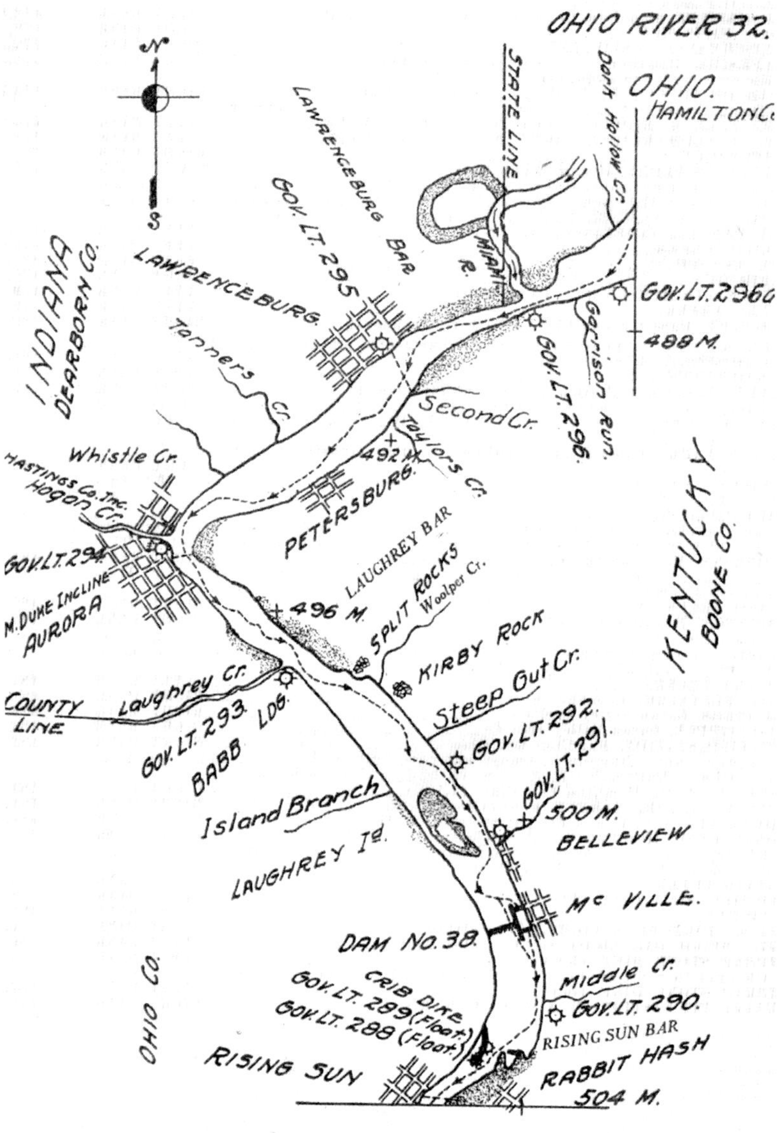

This Ohio River navigation chart is from Jones's *The Ohio River: Charts, Drawings and Description of Features Affecting Navigation* (circa 1916; rev. March 31, 1920, 2nd ed.). At the bottom of the page is Rising Sun, Indiana, on the right bank (left side of chart) and Rabbit Hash, Kentucky, on the left bank (right side of chart). Determination of the right and left banks of the river is made by beginning at Pittsburgh and traveling facing downstream; the bank on your right side is the right bank and that on your left side is the left bank. *From the author's personal collection.*

meandering Ohio. As they pushed on along the high ridge above the river, one of the men, seeking a shortcut around the tangles and stickers, made his way around the briars and closer to the bluff. His foot got tangled up in a vine, sending the runner tumbling toward the ground on his right side. But there was no ground, and he fell to his death seventy feet below through a narrow chasm that dissected the strange rocky conglomerate along which he was making his path. This happened to be Split Rock, a huge glacial outcropping that has been an Ohio River landmark since prehistoric times, formed by the last glacier activity twelve thousand years ago. The other soldier cautiously crawled over to the rocky death trap and, lying prone on the ground, realized that the bloody, pulpy mass resting on the rocks below was indeed lifeless. He snatched up the bag of gold, which by now was beginning to take a toll on the transporter. He and his burden continued downriver. He crossed Woolper Creek well above its mouth and stayed the course over the knobs. Eventually, he reached smoother, flatter terrain, but he was growing weary and winded, his pace slowing considerably.

At a place near where the present-day town of Bellevue (Belleview) Bottoms is located, the soldier came upon an Indian village on this fertile, level second-river terrace. Fortunately for him, all the male villagers were absent, composing a portion of the ambushing parties just upriver. Unfortunate

A vintage late-nineteenth/early twentieth-century postcard showing Split Rock on the Ohio River. Larger excursion boats would actually carry passengers to Split Rock and allow them the opportunity to get off and explore this Ohio River geological rarity and to hunt for emeralds, which were (erroneously) believed to be embedded in this glacial conglomerate rock. *From the author's personal collection.*

was the number of young boys playing in a simulated battle out on the flat with their bows and arrows. They spotted each other simultaneously, and the young warriors gave chase. Handicapped by his responsibility, the soldier was overtaken by the little braves, and they pummeled him with their arrows, ripping through his clothing. Three entered his body with such force that they were difficult to extract. But there was one that found its mark in proximity to his heart.

He struggled onward, and luckily his small pursuers gave up their chase. As the wounded soldier crossed Middle Creek (in the same spot where, thirty-two years later, Edward Meeks would locate the very first Boone County ferry), he grew markedly weaker and more feeble. But he regarded his charge as more precious than his life and struggled on, by now with seemingly purposeless ataxia. As he stumbled upon a certain oak tree, he finally collapsed into a pile of leaves, suffering, dehydrated, weak and delirious. He lay there as the events of the day rushed through his head, followed by his entire life, until the mercy of unconsciousness ended his suffering.

Enter the young Indian maiden. Seeing that death's hold had not yet prevailed, she lay the soldier's head in her lap and gently stroked his pale, clammy forehead, whispering gently, "White man hurt?" (So it wasn't Hollywood, after all, that propagated this stereotype!) His eyes flittered and eventually forced themselves open as he weakly patted the sack of gold next to him. "This bag not mine. Hide." With this, what little breath remained escaped in a final death moan, and he fell limp, eyes still open.

The Indian maiden pondered the scene, gently forced the dead soldier's eyes closed and repeated his last words over and over to herself until she realized it would be up to her to grant a dying man's final request. She took up the heavy sack, and instead of burying it right there under the oak tree, she carried it off some distance to a larger, mightier, more domineering oak—the matriarch of the forest—and buried it deep down amongst the roots, where it would remain safely hidden forever.

Nelson ends this part of the saga right here. He doesn't even tell the readers if the Indian maiden buried the dead hero. It is clear that the gold was the only protagonist in this story. At this point, he fast-forwards a number of years and focuses on a young man named Frank and a certain time in his life when he was walking home from New Orleans after deck-handing on a flatboat transporting produce to market downriver, got struck by a falling tree branch during a raging storm, broke his leg and was rescued by a band of friendly Indians and taken to their village, where he was doctored and nursed back to health by an old but obviously well-respected and prestigious squaw who just so happened to be the very Indian maiden who had buried the gold many, many years before. In talking to her, Frank determined, by the facts and descriptions in her story, that she had buried the treasure directly across the river from his hometown, Rising Sun, Indiana. As a matter of fact, he had marveled at times at that same giant oak tree on the opposite hillside. He healed up perfectly, left the motherly old squaw and the friendly villagers and made a beeline back to Indiana. His only stops were at taverns, as Frank had a propensity for the liquid spirits that gave them higher priority even than retrieving the buried gold.

By and large, Frank made it back home, where he lived a life that never relinquished his secret. He married, raised a large family and worked as a caulker down on the riverbank, picking up other odd river- and boat-related jobs along the way. He would work all day and then sneak across the river and dig all night under the two oak trees – because his pickled brain and faltering memory left him unsure about which tree exactly the aged squaw said she had buried the gold under.

Some townsfolk noticed a lonely, mysterious light in the hills across the river every night, like clockwork. Eventually, some of them ventured across to investigate, but by the time they arrived, the light would be extinguished and nothing unusual discovered. But the unexplained phenomenon soon became a favorite topic of conversation amongst the townspeople. As Nelson noted, "Some thought it was a jack o'lantern, some averred it was a comet; while others, susceptible to ghostly influences, were afraid it was a ha'nt."

It seems that whenever Frank was involved in these conversations, he would successfully talk it down without giving so much as a clue that his involvement was key. Eventually frustrated by dead-ends, the townsfolk gave it up, and "the subject passed into the limbo of ungratified though insatiable curiosity." But the nightly visits continued for years and years, and Frank's behavior and physical condition suffered from the continuous lack of sleep and his self-induced state of embalmment. His ever-growing family, his acquaintances and neighbors and even strangers who did not know him but took note of his rituals, were flabbergasted when Frank eventually purchased that very same Kentucky hillside across the river that was home to the two oak trees in question. "How could he have even begun to save enough money for the land purchase, considering his financial obligations to support that growing number of family members and needs, not to mention his now-daily intake of corn distillate?" they wondered out loud. Nelson added, "No one suspected that he had a hidden store upon which to draw as necessity required." The question remains today: did he really have such a store?

"Did Frank ever show, by word or deed, that he was possessed of a great secret?" Nelson asks rhetorically in his tale. He doesn't offer an answer. He just adds that at some point later, one of the more prominent elders and old-timers of the neighborhood was passing Frank's house one day when he was aroused by a pitiful, weakly voice calling out his name. Nelson mentions that the old-timer summoned in this manner was a man "who has been elected to many offices of honor and trust of old Boone, and who Frank looked up to and greatly admired." Nelson could only have been speaking of James A. Wilson, of course, the original proprietor of the Rabbit Hash General Store.

As the story continues, this person, upon investigating the feeble cries for assistance, found Frank lying prone on the ground with an obvious compounded fracture of the leg. An emergency amputation of the affected extremity was performed by a local surgeon, but it was soon discovered that the operation would be to no avail, and the patient was surely doomed. The comfort giver remained at Frank's bedside for the purpose of assisting him in a painless as possible final transition. When the time was nigh and the death rattle ominous, the dying man signaled to his old friend to lean his ear to the victim's lips, which he did. As Frank's failing spirit tried to muster one last statement, all that surfaced were the words: "Big oak." And to this day, the question remains: did Frank find the buried treasure of Rabbit Hash?

After leaving the reader in complete suspense and wondering if all that gold had really been found, Nelson changes the subject and skips to a small addended article at the end of his booklet to answer yet a different question. This article is entitled "Rabbit Hash, Kentucky: The Origin of Its Name."

The setting for the story was the winter of 1847, around Christmastime and during very high water. It was cold, and a deep accumulation of snow covered the ground as a group of area residents peered out into the rapid-running river and watched buildings, livestock, trees, haystacks, lumber and crops being swept down the churning brown waters of the Ohio. They were not engaging in the happy and joyous conversations that one would expect to hear this time of year. Instead, a shroud of gloom and suffering dominated their discourse. As they were witnessing the great destruction and lamenting their losses, the topic of conversation turned to what each family would be serving for their holiday dinners. As each one present took his turn, the main meat entrees included goose, a fat hen, fresh pork and others. Finally, there was but one remaining testimony, and that was from the town jester or comedian. His name was Frank. As he looked around the landscape and observed all the low-dwelling wildlife being driven upland and inland by the ever-rising river level, he responded that it looked to him like there would be plenty of rabbit hash this season. His remark brought smiles to those around him and broke the sullen mood. From that point on, Frank's personal nickname around the community became "Rabbit Hash." Eventually, that moniker bled over to become the preferred and endearing name of the small Ohio River community.

Throughout the second and third quarters of the nineteenth century, most of the mail traveled up and down the river system by way of steamboat. There seemed to be an ever-increasing frequency of mail destined for Carlton (Ohio River Mile #504) winding up in Carrollton, just thirty nine miles downriver (Ohio River Mile #543) and vice versa. Since Carrollton was by far the larger of the two towns, the postal service asked Carlton residents to choose a new name for their post office. Since they had been referring to the place for years as Rabbit Hash, it was a no-brainer. Rabbit Hash would be the official name of the town, and it would have its own postmark and post office to prove it.

In 1894, the famous historian Reuben Gold Thwaites, with his wife and a friend, made an excursion down the Ohio and Mississippi Rivers from Pittsburgh to New Orleans in a couple of small wooden boats. In his journal, which was eventually published as the book *Afloat on the Ohio*, he records his stop at Rabbit Hash, where he took advantage of the postal services there to send out his mail. He visited for a while and interviewed some of the locals. He even had the courtesy to leave us with photographic evidence of the Wilson and Riddell (Rabbit Hash) general store and the horse-powered ferryboat that operated between Rabbit Hash and Rising Sun, Indiana.

Horse-powered ferryboats were actually quite common in the United States throughout the nineteenth century on inland streams and small rivers. Commonly referred to as "horseboats," these craft were not very popular or utilized in European cultures but were quite the rage in the transportation systems of the American frontier. They were perfectly suited for small streams and rivers and were relatively easy to operate and maintain. The machinery was simple and sturdy, consisting of a treadmill for the horse(s) connected to a series of gears and shafts to a side-wheel and a tiller, or sweep, mounted at the stern for steering.

Since there was a paucity of bridges spanning the Ohio along its 981-mile length, horseboat ferries were commonly found at every small river community, especially if there was a similar small river community across the water. The ferry fees were usually a standard charge, as set up by the county court, depending on what was ferried across. There was a flat fee for a pedestrian, and then the fee increased according to the type of conveyance

A horseboat ferry landed on the Rabbit Hash shore, waiting for passengers. "Uncle" Bill Stephens is standing. The boy is unidentified. *From the Rabbit Hash Historical Society collection.*

hauled across, usually based on the number of wheels. Fees were higher for the number of horses or oxen pulling the conveyance. For herds of sheep, cattle or pigs, it was based on price per head.

At ferry crossings that were fairly busy all day long, the horseboat made back-to-back trips on a regular schedule. For those not so busy, there was a large farm bell mounted at each landing for the passengers to call the boat over. Gunshots in the air also served as appropriate signals. The operator of the Rabbit Hash/Rising Sun ferry typically had a vegetable garden at each landing, upland from the shore, to which he attended daily. The produce supplemented his horseboat income. These gardens were said to be the very best in the county. Small barns with stalls on the Rabbit Hash side of the river housed the horsepower each night, and fuel was relatively inexpensive. The barn also served as the ferry operator's business office. In Rabbit Hash, the ferry landing can still be easily discerned in the present-day landscape. What is known as the "ferry lot" on deeds and property descriptions is the area next to the general store on the river side.

In the early years of James A. Wilson, the ferry operator and the proprietor of the general store were the same person. As both enterprises grew, it took

A horse and wagon loading onto a horse-powered ferryboat on the Rabbit Hash side of the Ohio River with Rising Sun in the background. Note the low-water stage of the river in this photo. *From the Rabbit Hash Historical Society collection, obtained originally from the Ohio County, Indiana Historical Society collection.*

separate individuals to man both businesses. Not uncommonly, the same person owned both and simply hired or leased one or the other business to a partner. In the later years, both were owned by separate individuals or group of partners. Regardless of the owners, both the store and the ferry were always known by the prefix "Rabbit Hash."

An old belief that was always repeated was that the ferry owners would only use blind horses to power the horseboat. The reason for this was that a blind horse wouldn't get spooked by the water, current and waves. But Robert Haydon Wilson, the grandson of James A., explained, "That's a bunch of bunk. The horses were initially normal healthy horses. It was the constant glare of the sun on the river day after day that eventually made them go blind."

Throughout the town's long and varied history, the store and the ferry had generally remained the two constants. Next in line were the blacksmith and the doctor, both of which occupied specified locations within the town proper. The blacksmith played a key role in a rural river town like Rabbit Hash. Consisting primarily of yeoman farmers and rivermen, the area kept him busy making repairs on tools, farming implements, conveyances and the horse-powered ferryboats and other river craft. He also shod the beasts of burden and fabricated all sorts of household items and necessary parts and pieces. The blacksmith shop was generally located on the bank, adjacent to the ferry lot. The coal lot sat right next to it. Archaeological artifacts identified these sites when footers were dug for the Rabbit Hash Museum, which now occupies the site.

Smith Riggs was one of the last local smiths to operate there. As a matter of fact, he also had another shop across the river on the Rising Sun bank. He was in great demand because he was such a craftsman, not only working with iron but with wood as well. He was practicing his trade from the early 1880s up until the 1930s. A newspaper article in the *Rising Sun Recorder*, dated 1928, featured an article about Smith Riggs, but it was in the dubious honor vein. Its heading read: "Satisfies Conscience Before Taking Work."

> *From the seclusion and obscurity of his quaint little blacksmith shop in the quiet and peaceful village of Rising Sun, Ind., which boasts one "movie" and where it still is possible to rent a four-room house with a garage for $10 a month, Smith Riggs, 65, for nearly half a century "a jolly coppersmith* [sic]*," has emerged into the center of the public eye.*
>
> *Quite by accident, Riggs, a quiet, unassuming, church-going and God-fearing man who can hammer the most fantastic designs from iron at white heat on an anvil, is occupying this position.*
>
> *Modern civilization has singled him out from the 120,000,000 persons, more or less, in the United States, to fashion a dread instrument of death—an electric chair, or rather two electric chairs, which ironically are classified as "more humane" than those now in common use.*

One of two electric chairs fabricated by blacksmith Smith Riggs, who operated a blacksmith shop in both Rising Sun and Rabbit Hash. These chairs were made for use in two penitentiaries in the state of Illinois. *From the Rabbit Hash Historical Society collection.*

The new type of chair…will lessen the time required to strap a doomed man into the chair preparatory to his electrocution…Ordinarily it has required from five to ten minutes to strap a man into the chair. Less than one minute will be required for the same procedure in the new chair.

Clamps, which can be shut in the twinkling of an eye, will replace straps on the new chairs. Everything will be done to make the occupant of the chair comfortable. Even an adjustable reclining back has been included.

It was with great reluctance that Riggs accepted the contract for the construction of the two chairs… "It cost me one whole night's sleep to make up my mind about constructing the chairs," Riggs said… "I laid awake all that night thinking about them. I thought what a terrible thing it would be if an innocent man would be electrocuted in one of them. Then I thought of the many innocent persons who are murdered in cold blood each year. All night long these thoughts ran through my mind. Finally I decided…the next day that I would make them."

One of the chairs, when completed, will go to the Joliet, Ill., penitentiary; the other will go to the penitentiary at Maynard, Ill…Riggs has engaged Ernest Williamson, carpenter, to make the wooden framework of the chair. When the word spread through the little village, which is situated about forty-eight miles below Cincinnati, the entire population of some 1,500 was thrown into a hub-bub of excitement.

Riggs's little shop became the object of all eyes. Some persons shook their heads and did not hesitate to state their opposition. The majority took the broader view.

Someone has to do it, says Riggs.

Smith Riggs lived in Rabbit Hash. He died on November 14, 1936, just two short months before his ingenious rods-and-hooks system kept the Rabbit Hash General Store firmly secured under eighty-plus feet of Ohio River floodwater. He is buried in the East Bend Methodist Church Cemetery.

The other well-established profession of some longevity in the town was that of the local physician. Rabbit Hash has had upwards of five or six different medical doctors in the immediate vicinity throughout its many years. They were mostly short-lived practices for some reason or other, but their presence was always appreciated and enjoyed.

The doctor's office was located across the road from the blacksmith shop. It was a small two-room wooden structure and served several different physicians over the years. Four houses downriver from that was the local physicians' residence. Dr. Lewis C. Cohen and Dr. Ivan Earle Carlyle were the two doctors most remembered, and they both lived in that residence and practiced in that office. The 1883 *Boone County Atlas* lists Dr. Cohen as a practicing physician in Rabbit Hash. Dr. Cohen was born in Burlington on November 12, 1848, the son of Samuel and Marie A. Cohen. He was raised and educated in Burlington in the public schools. He next attended Ohio Medical College and augmented his medical education in New York, Philadelphia and Baltimore. He practiced medicine in Rabbit Hash for twenty-seven years, from 1874 until 1901, at which time he retired and moved across the river to Rising Sun, where he lived for another twenty-nine years. On October 18, 1877, he married Jennie Hastings, the daughter of Mr. and Mrs. James Hastings, who lived just about four miles downriver from Rabbit Hash where her father's farm was located. This probably explains how Dr. Cohen winded up practicing in Rabbit Hash. Dr. and Mrs. Cohen had no children. She died in the year 1928 and he in the following year. Dr. Cohen was a member of numerous medical associations and societies. He was also a Mason; a member of the Knights of Pythius, which had a large two-story meeting hall just a few houses upriver from the Rabbit Hash General Store;

A view of the rear of the East Bend Methodist Episcopal Church showing the remnants of the exterior stairway landing to the second floor IOOF Lodge meeting hall until an 1894 tornado took off the second story of the structure. Note the newer-looking mismatched bricks forming the repaired gable end of the church, now a one-story building. *Photo by Callie Clare.*

and a member of the Independent Order of Odd Fellows, which met on the second floor of the East Bend Methodist Church until a late 1880s tornado took that story off. The church was then repaired without the second floor and appeared just as it does today. Many of his patients remembered Dr. Cohen's favorite motto: "Do right because it is right to do right."

At some point after 1901, there was a Dr. L. Frank Hopkins, MD, practicing in the small doctor's office in Rabbit Hash. There is not much known or recorded about this particular Rabbit Hash physician. His practice was taken over by Dr. Ivan Earle Carlyle in 1909, when he purchased the office from Dr. Hopkins for $400. His tour of duty as the town doc lasted up until 1924, when he and his family moved to Sedalia, Illinois, where he opened another practice.

One of the catalogued artifacts in the Rabbit Hash Historical Society is Dr. Carlyle's "baby book," which lists every baby he delivered in Rabbit Hash, along with the parents' names and other vital statistics. It's quite a telling tribute to the good doctor to see how many of the babies had Ivan or Earle in their listed given names. Ivan Earle Carlyle was born on February 22, 1882, in Scott County, Indiana. He attended school in Scottsburg, Indiana, and graduated from Borden College in Borden, Indiana, with a BS degree. He taught all twelve grades in both Scott and Marion Counties in Indiana. He married Della McCoskey in 1903. Their first child, Harry, was born on June 11, 1905 (his twin sister died at childbirth). In 1907, their second

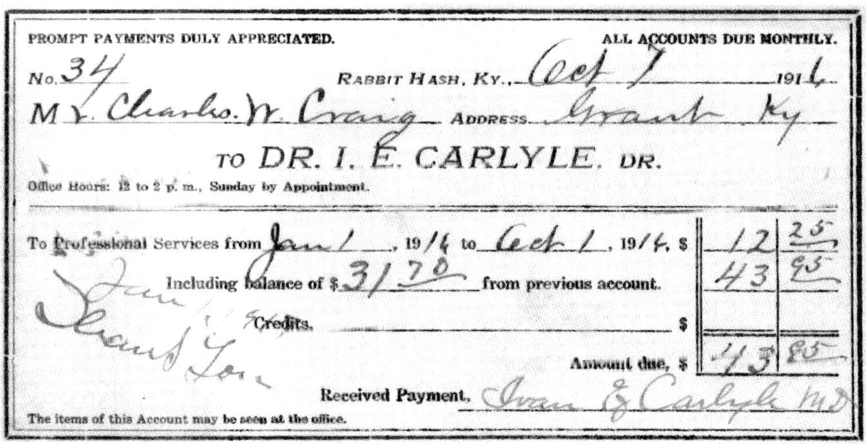
PROMPT PAYMENTS DULY APPRECIATED. ALL ACCOUNTS DUE MONTHLY.
No. 34 RABBIT HASH, KY., Oct 1 1916
Mr. Charles W. Craig ADDRESS Grant Ky
TO DR. I. E. CARLYLE, DR.
Office Hours: 12 to 2 p. m., Sunday by Appointment.
To Professional Services from Jan 1, 1916 to Oct 1, 1916 $ 12 25
Including balance of $31.70 from previous account. 43 95
Credits. $
Amount due, $ 43 95
Received Payment, Ivan E Carlyle MD
The items of this Account may be seen at the office.

A receipt from Dr. Ivan E. Carlisle for payment received from C.W. Craig, marked "Rabbit Hash, Ky., Oct. 1, 1916." Dr. Carlisle took over Dr. Hopkins's practice in 1912. *From the Rabbit Hash Historical Society collection (donated by Lib Stephens).*

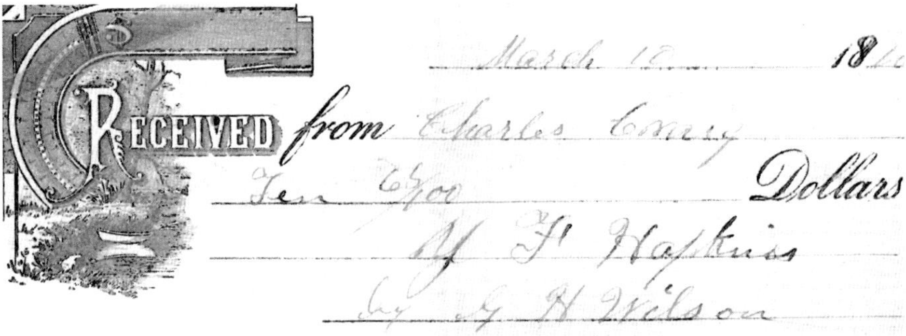
March 18
Received from Charles Craig
Ten 00 Dollars
Y F Hopkins
by G H Wilson

Dr. Hopkins practiced medicine in Rabbit Hash before Dr. Carlisle arrived in 1912. Here is a receipt from Dr. Y.F. Hopkins for payment collected from C.W. Craig. *From the Rabbit Hash Historical Society collection (donated by Lib Stephens).*

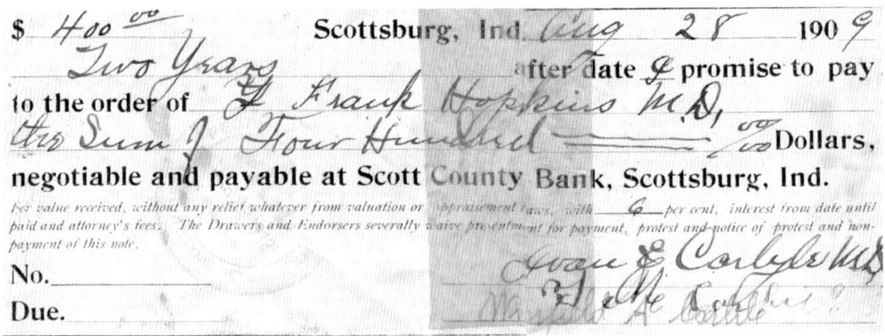
$ 400 00 Scottsburg, Ind. Aug 28 1909

Two Years after date I promise to pay

to the order of Y Frank Hopkins M.D.,

the Sum of Four Hundred 00/100 Dollars,

negotiable and payable at Scott County Bank, Scottsburg, Ind.

For value received, without any relief whatever from valuation or appraisement laws, with 6 per cent. interest from date until paid and attorney's fees. The Drawers and Endorsers severally waive presentment for payment, protest and notice of protest and non-payment of this note.

No.

Due.

Ivan E Carlyle MD

A promissory note from Dr. Carlisle made out to Dr. Hopkins for the purchase of his doctor's office and practice in Rabbit Hash, dated 1909. *From the Rabbit Hash Historical Society collection.*

child, Ruth, was born at Juliette, Indiana, where Dr. Carlyle was teaching his last year of school. During the time he taught school, he was also studying medicine at the University of Louisville, which was due south and across the river in Kentucky. He graduated with his MD in 1908 and practiced for one year in New Philadelphia, Indiana, before coming to Rabbit Hash.

After Dr. Carlyle, records are again scant, but local history verifies that other doctors practiced in Rabbit Hash; some were alleged to have been from Rising Sun, keeping offices in both towns and commuting by ferry. In the 1930s, there was a Dr. Shallenberger at some point, but not much other information is known about him. No matter which doctor was in residence in any particular year, house calls were always made for those unable to get to the offices for treatment of their maladies. After the 1930s, folks recall that

Dr. Ivan Earle Carlisle sitting in his buggy in front of his home in Rabbit Hash with his team of horses ready to "go out the road [*sic*]." House calls were a major part of a rural doctor's routine, and he had to have dependable horses and a good buggy always available. *From the Rabbit Hash Historical Society collection.*

the doctor's office was used for a barbershop when Rube Kirtley cut hair in between his farming duties.

In a personal interview in 1994, local lifelong resident, Wanetta Clause, gave a detailed description of the town of Rabbit Hash in the early 1930s before the "big" flood of 1937. She had a tremendous memory, which was accented with acute detail. Beginning with the general store, she described the entire area, building by building, on both sides of the road. Adjacent to the store and between it and the ferry landing was a vacant lot that was always known as the store lot. It served many purposes, from a staging area for goods to be loaded onto the ferry to be transported across the river to waiting steamboats, to a parking area for wagons and carts awaiting ferriage, to a picnic area, horseshoe throwing pits and, in Wanetta's youth, a croquet field. Where the barn is now, on the river side of the road, was the creamery operated by Jack Acra. Wanetta's mother, Ada Acra Ryle, kept the books for her brother's business. Next to this, going downriver, was Miss Teemie Stephens's house. She had a huge square grand piano, which had to be moved to higher ground every time the Ohio threatened to flood. She was a spinster whom a lot of people "thought wasn't quite right."

Next to Teemy was a garage-type building in which the Ryle brothers stored their huckster truck. "Uncle Jack Acra ran the huckster truck for them." This building was rebuilt in the same spot after the '37 flood out of salvaged materials from buildings farther upriver. Next to this sat a long narrow building—the tobacco warehouse. There was an old bachelor by the name of At Holmes who lived in this building, but Wanetta did not recall his reason for living there. She assumed he "watched the place." In a similar handwritten history by "old Bill Stephens" in 1981, Stephens recalled that the man was named Philip Holmes and he lived there in a two-story apartment in the front of the tobacco warehouse; he had a plowshare and blacksmith shop a little farther down the road. According to Stephens, Mr. Holmes "made the best horse plows that was made at that time." Continuing down the road on the river side were barns, carriage houses and other outbuildings of different functions, all of which were part of the homes and small farms across the road from them. Behind all this were extensive cornfields all the way down to the river's edge. Every one of these structures was a victim of the '37 flood. Nothing stood on that side of the road when the waters finally subsided.

This scene shows the old creamery station and scales in the March 1933 flood. The milk collected from the surrounding local dairy farms was weighed and processed here for shipment to Cincinnati. This structure, too, would be taken by the floodwaters of 1937. *From the Rabbit Hash Historical Society collection.*

A real-photo postcard entitled "High Water Rabbit Hash, Kentucky opposite Rising Sun, February, 1907." Note the general store in the far lower left at the water's edge. *From the author's personal collection.*

On the other side of the road, beginning again at the Rabbit Hash General Store, across the road and up on a small hill was the Ryle Brothers Store. It was a feed and seed store that dealt in hardware and farm implements, as well as other things. "Dickie Stephens worked there and tested eggs and weighed chickens." Clayton and John Ryle apparently also dealt with poultry and eggs at one time, as Bill Stephens recalled. This is the same building as the current Rabbit Hash Ironworks where the Elk Creek Winery tasting room is located. An interesting aside about this building is the fact that about 1910, a basement was dug out under the building, and homemade hand-mixed concrete was used to build the basement walls, using old scraps of iron and old parts from farming implements as reinforcing steel. At times, this basement was used as a Model T Ford dealership, a pool hall and a pork-processing and packing business. It is rumored that during Prohibition, bottles of whiskey could be purchased there as well, "as long as you were a local." (This is really more of a fact than a rumor.) Later on, this building housed the Stephens Grocery when Rabbit Hash sported two general stores.

Just below the hill from this Ryle Brothers feed and implement store, directly across the road from the general store, was another Ryle Brothers business that was basically a gas station. Two gas pumps sat beside the building, and oil and other automotive needs were available in the store,

View from the porch of Craig's general store looking downriver as the floodwaters of 1937 begin to creep into position. This would prove to be the last time this particular view would ever be enjoyed, as all the buildings on the right side of the road were later washed away, and the one on the left floated up into the woods, where it was tied off and later added to the rear of the building above it (not shown). *From the Rabbit Hash Historical Society collection.*

These two stores would become one after the '37 flood. The store building in the foreground was floated off its foundation and into the woods beyond where it was tied off with ropes. After the flood, it was attached, rear to rear, to the other store building above it and to the left of the photo. The "new" building thus had two front façades. It currently serves as a wine shop and tasting room in the front and a bed-and-breakfast in the back. *From the Rabbit Hash Historical Society collection.*

The doctor's house as the 1937 floodwaters were about to crest at the official Cincinnati reading of 79.9 feet (over 81.0 feet in Lawrenceburg, Indiana), with the water lapping at the front porch steps. Notice the small barns and outbuildings in the center of the photo. These were located on the opposite side of the road and would be swept away by the floodwaters before all was said and done. The house behind the doctor's is the Palmers House, which also survived and would later be owned by Edna Flower, the $250,000 benefactor of the Rabbit Hash Historical Society. *From the Rabbit Hash Historical Society collection.*

A photograph taken by Clayton Ryle of his gas station and automotive store after the 1937 flood floated it off of its foundation and replaced it higher up the bank. *From the Rabbit Hash Historical Society collection.*

along with other sundry items that may appeal to the motorist. It's hard to tell what was carried as stock. When all was said and done with the '37 flood, this entire building was floated off its foundation by the floodwaters and conveniently turned around and relocated in the woods behind and in between the Ryle Brothers Store and the doctor's office. The townsmen tied off the building with ropes and later tacked it to the rear of the other Ryle Brothers building, butt to butt, to create the very long and skinny structure that is there today. It's the building with two fronts, one being the winery and the other the Hashienda.

Continuing on down this side of the road, the next structure is the doctor's office. To its left and up the hill sits what is locally known as the Carlton House. "This is where Frank and Ora Belle Green lived," recalled Wanetta. Next to it was a two-story frame farmhouse (no longer standing due to a fire in the 1980s) in which John and Stella Ryle lived. Before their house occupied this spot, Lewis Lunsford Stephens, a brief partner of Cal Riddell, lived on the same site in a different structure. Next to this on its left was Clayton and Wilma Ryle's two-story frame house, which is still standing. A previous residence also occupied this spot but burned down around 1899 or 1900. It was the home of Ben Calvert, who worked for many years at the general store as a clerk and druggist. Next was the doctor's residence, also still standing. It is a two-story frame home with lots of gingerbread—an

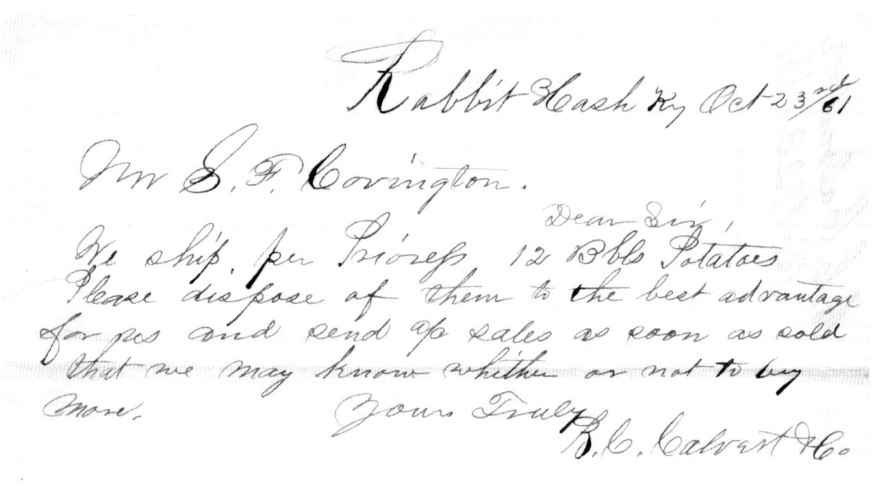

Rabbit Hash Ky Oct 23rd/61

Mr S. F. Covington.

Dear Sir,

We ship, per Progress, 12 Bbls Potatoes

Please dispose of them to the best advantage

for us and send a/c sales as soon as sold

that we may know whether or not to buy

more.

Yours Truly

B.C. Calvert & Co

An early handwritten letter from B.C. Calvert, signed and dated Rabbit Hash, Kentucky, 1861. Calvert at one time was a clerk and a druggist in the Wilson general store and most likely was a business partner of James A. Wilson before Cal Riddell came on the scene. *From author's personal collection.*

impressive sight in its day. When the last doctor left town, the house was purchased by John and Alice Palmer, who also owned the home to the left of it. Wanetta goes on to say that she purchased this place from the Palmers, eventually selling it to a Mr. Fresney. The second Palmer house became a haberdashery where Mrs. Palmer sold hats. This is the house that was later purchased and owned by Edna Flowers, who bequeathed a gift of a quarter-million dollars to the Rabbit Hash Historical Society.

The next property is the former home of Charles W. and Emma Craig, who owned and operated the Rabbit Hash General Store from 1919 until Charles's death in 1945. After that, the store remained in the name of Miss Emma and was operated first by her son, Sheeny, into the 1960s and then by her daughter, Lib (Pearl Elizabeth), and her husband, Cliff Stephens, until they sold it to Louie Scott in 1978. To the left of the house sat the "dog barn," which was utilized by Sheeny when he was the county dogcatcher. This barn still remains. Another barn was just across the road, but only its foundation remains. To the left of the dog barn was a small two-room shack. "Poor people rented it," Wanetta recalled, but she could not remember their names. Little Ranty Creek was next. On the other side of the creek was a small wooden-frame farmhouse owned by Willie and Vida Stephens, who farmed the property on both sides of the road. The next property was

The Craig family barn in the March 1933 Ohio River flood. As county dog warden, this is where Sheeny Craig kept the dogs he caught. *From the Rabbit Hash Historical Society collection.*

significantly farther down the road back in the 1930s. Today, it is known as Earl Locke's place. It, too, was a small hillside farm. Another family of Ryles lived there—Lucy Stephens Ryle and Filmore Ryle. They had three sons and two daughters. One of the sons, Shelby Lee Ryle, died of pneumonia on the very day Wanetta was born in 1922. She was named Wanetta Lee in his honor. The other two sons, Clarence and Kenneth, became veterinarians. Clarence Ryle specialized in racehorse veterinary medicine and practiced in Georgetown and Lexington. Kenneth Ryle practiced in Boone County. They both married Stephens girls. One sister was Alberta Ryle, who married Bluford Clore, and they lived upriver from Rabbit Hash in the same house where Lib and Cliff Stephens retired. The other sister was Hetha Ryle. She married Wilbur Kelly, and they lived in Burlington. Big Ranty Creek runs through this farm to enter into the Ohio River.

Beyond this were others small farms. Charlie and Jessie Wilson lived in the place currently owned by Charlie Hotchkiss. Next came the farm of William and Ethyl Stephens. Also living there was Bill's bachelor brother, Lewis "Punk" Stephens, who died there in the 1880s. The house was originally a two-pen dogtrot log house, presumably built by Andy Dolph, who was a well-respected and noted carpenter in the area. In a typed history of East Bend Methodist Church was found a handwritten note that stated:

> *In 1860 Andrew Jackson Dolph moved from Rising Sun, Indiana to Rabbit Hash, Ky and settled with his family. He was a carpenter by trade and interested in the construction of a Methodist Meeting House and Odd Fellows Lodge Hall in one building.*
>
> *The ground had been donated by deed from Wm. and Nancy Neal August 15, 1860. The size of the piece of land was 1 acre…deeded to Trustees of Methodist Episcopal Church South to be used for a meeting house and Public Graveyard.*
>
> *All woodwork was hand made by Mr. Andrew Jackson Dolph. In 1893 the 2nd story or* [Lodge Hall] *was removed and Church was remodeled.*

A *Boone County Recorder* article dated December 17, 1894, stated, "East Bend Methodist Church which suffered so much damage by a wind storm in July last has been thoroughly repaired and painted, and is now one of the handsomest churches in the county."

In addition to the "red" church, Dolph is credited with building several of the houses in the area along the Ohio River. He built Miss Emma Craig's house and the Knights of Pythius Hall, as well as others. Andy Dolph's house still remains but has undergone extensive renovation, including the removal of the original log walls.

The next farm was that of Frank and Edith Cunningham. Frank at one time owned and operated the Rabbit Hash ferry. The Cunninghams also owned a farm in Rising Sun and eventually moved across the river. The farm was at one time leased to Sheeny Craig, who logged the back portion for timber and actually sold off a portion near the river even though he didn't own the land. It was later purchased and farmed by Beulah and Leonard Riggs. Beulah remained there for another twenty years or so after Leonard's death. She kept her house and an acre and sold the remainder to the current owners.

Again, the Ryle, Stephens, Wilson, Craig, Acra and other common Rabbit Hash surnames make their presence up and down this small town along the river.

An East Bend Lodge No. 114, Knights of Pythius, Rabbit Hash, Kentucky pin-back ribbon badge. *From the Rabbit Hash Historical Society collection.*

6

FROM GENERATION TO GENERATION

It is an established historical fact that the Ohio River played a major role in the settlement patterns of Boone County, Kentucky, in general and Rabbit Hash in particular. Families with all their worldly possessions on a flatboat or barge migrated downriver to their intended destinations, which sometimes would be right where the boat wrecked, sank or deteriorated. They settled along the river and up its many tributaries, seeking out the most suitable sites for their survival and subsistence needs. Just like the natives before them, they looked for fertile croplands, sources of fresh water, plentiful game and good hunting and fishing. They avoided the unhealthy swamp ground and looked for high and dry topography with good air circulation to locate their homesites.

Other early pioneer settlers arrived in Boone County via the Cumberland Gap and the Wilderness Road. Many of the old roads were former deer and buffalo paths or Indian trails following creeks, rivers and ridges and remain the origins of the roads still being used today throughout the country. Boone County's early settlers were really yeoman (occupying a position between gentleman and laborer) farmers, just as Thomas Jefferson had envisioned would populate every available acre in his "empire for liberty." They would work and improve their own land and raise enough to sustain their family with some left over for sale or barter. Farm produce would make its way to the river, where it would be loaded onto flatboats and later onto steamboats or ferried across the river to awaiting markets. Manufactured goods would arrive in the reverse manner.

Boone County has remained predominately agricultural and rural for most of its history, and since before the Civil War, hemp, grains and tobacco had been the main sustaining cash crops. Even commercial occupations such as sawmill or gristmill operators or blacksmiths basically served the agricultural community. It wasn't until the second third of the twentieth century that things in Boone County really began to shift from an agrarian focus to one with a manufacturing, industrial and service-oriented complexion. The real metamorphosis began in the 1940s with the Greater Cincinnati Airport's growth, along with the construction of the major interstate highway systems I-75, I-71 and I-275, which began in the early 1960s and continued through the 1970s. Once again, lifestyles and culture changed in direct response to transportation modes and advances.

But Rabbit Hash had always been a product of the river. It was never changed or affected by railroads, airplanes or interstate. It literally lived and died by the river from the time of its first settlers. These bold and daring families came from all over the thirteen established states, seeking out personal or familial land grants and patents or hoping to claim, purchase, squat or homestead parcels of ground. They may have been motivated by the promise of the most fertile ground ever cultivated or simply trying to escape the overused, poorly nutritious and highly eroded croplands of their former situations. Maybe they were simply adventurous, or maybe they were attempting to escape from someone, someplace or something. Regardless of the reasons people were populating this middle Ohio River Valley, they liked what they found here and were willing to lay the foundations of their family names for generation after generation to build on.

There remain to this day, in and around Rabbit Hash and its environs, many of the first-generation surnames. Names like Ryle, Marshall, Hogan, Scott, Kendall, Berkshire, Parker, Cooper, Lee and Millers from North Carolina and Stephens, Craig, Hawkins, Rice, Smith, Brady, Wilson, Kirtley and Calvert from Virginia were among the first immigrant family names in the area. Over time, many of these names became diluted in the subsequent flood of others. Some left the area headed for other destinations to place their roots and establish their family legacies. But a few of these family names are still very much alive and well in the Rabbit Hash neighborhood. Others like Piatt, Grant, Dinsmore, Gaines, Clore, Walton, Huey and Rogers still have namesake reminders around the area. The same can be said for the Hodges family; the Louden and Feldhaus families; and the Botts, Riddell, Acra, Neal, Presser, Aylor, Douglass and Brown surnames. But on top of the family name list in this portion of Boone County, Kentucky, belong the Ryles and Stephenses.

THE RYLE FAMILY

Probably the two most prominent, established family names that consistently and repeatedly come up when speaking of the comprehensive past of Rabbit Hash, Kentucky, are the Ryles and the Stephenses. When the Ryles first arrived in Boone County, Kentucky, they settled at Tanner's Station (now Petersburg), on the banks of the Ohio River at Ohio River Mile #493, across from the mouth of Tanner's Creek. Some Ryle family historians say this was as early as 1792, the year Kentucky was granted its statehood. Others say it was as late as 1804. It was probably not this late but somewhere in between the two dates. The patriarch, John Ryle, died in North Carolina in 1777 at a fairly young age. His cause of death is not known, but it is not believed that it was related to the onset of the war against Great Britain because, according to Herbert E. Ryle (author of *The Stephens/Ryle Families*), some oral family history traditions hold that the Ryles were forced to leave North Carolina for refusing to take up arms against the mother country. This refusal to fight against the British is probably accurate. John Ryle "took the oath" back in 1769, pledging his allegiance to the king; he swore to never bear arms against him or risk the punishment of death without trial. But Herbert Ryle doesn't think that's why the Ryles left North Carolina. He says, "John Ryle died at the very beginning of the war, and his sons were really not old enough to have fought. It is more likely they had the same reasons for leaving as did thousands of other North Carolinians and Virginians." He goes on to say that even before 1776, there were groups of men from Anson County, North Carolina, "who were attracted to the unsettled and unexplored lands lying west of the Appalachians," where they spent months on end hunting and trapping and then building their own rafts, which transported their goods downriver to sell at the New Orleans markets. From there, they would book passage on a ship back to the coast of North Carolina and begin the process all over again. Obviously, this account parallels the exploits of Daniel Boone and his "longhunter" trips into Kentucky after his family left Pennsylvania to settle in western North Carolina.

John Ryle's will provided that each of his six children receive a bed and a slave, along with an equal portion of his land. His wife was lent his landholding, totaling four hundred acres, which would eventually be divided among the four sons and the two daughters (Elizabeth, the eldest, and Mary, the youngest). The boys eventually all sold their lands "in separate transactions from September 14, 1793 to April 23, 1795. John Ryle, Jr. was the first to sell his land. The oldest son, James Ryle, was the last," presumably after the deaths of his mother and his sister Elizabeth. Herbert Ryle regrets that nothing else is known about John Ryle Sr.'s widow, not even her name. He speculates, however, that she was a Larkin or a Whitmill, since she gave these names to two of her sons. Another possibility was that she was a Harrington, as this name shows up numerous times in future generations. "There was a man in Anson County records named Whitmill Harrington, but we cannot connect him to the family."

The last will of John Ryle of Anson County is found in Will Book A, one of the few remaining extant books from this early North Carolina county. It is reported that most of the other records and court accounts were tragically destroyed during the Civil War. It is important to include Ryle's will here, as it not only clearly lists his heirs and enumerates what he felt was important to pass on to them, but it also speaks volumes of a slaveholding family where human chattel was equally as important and valuable as real estate. In this rare case, the slaves were named, thereby giving them an identity and a genealogy.

John Ryle's Will

In the name of God, Amen, I, John Ryle, of Anson County in the province of North Carolina, being weak of body but of sound memory, thanks be to God for the same, Calling to Mind the mortality of the body and knowing that it is appointed for all men once to die do make and ordain this my last will and Testament. That is to say Principally and first of all I give and recommend my soul to the hand of Almighty God that gave it and my body I recommend to the Earth to be buried in a Decent Christian burial at the Descretion of my Executors, nothing doubting but at the General Resurrection I shall receive the same again by the mighty power of God, and as touching such worldly estate wherewith it has pleased God to bless me in this life I give, devise, and dispose of the same in the following manner and form, etc.

Item: First I give my son, James, one negro, March.

Item: I give my daughter, Elizabeth, one Negro, Moll.

Item: I give unto my son, John, one Negro named Harry.

Item: I leave one negro, Jack, to be sold at the discretion of my wife and the money arising from the sale to purchase a young negro for my son, Whitmill.

Item: I give unto my son, Larkin, one negro named Esses.

Item: I give unto my daughter, Mary, one Negro named Fillem.

Item: I give unto my six children each of them one bed and furniture and I give unto my son, James, one shot gun.

Item: I give all my land to be equally divided among my six children to them and their assigns forever and if either of them should lose their negro before they come of age that they should have a young negro purchased out of the value of my lands or other effects.
Item: I lend unto my loving wife my whole estate, Goods, and Chattels in during her widowhood and if my wife should marry I lend her my house and fifty acres of land in during her life and my other Estate to be divided according to my Will and appoint my wife Executor and my son, James, Executor, and do hereby acknowledge this my last Will and Testament.

John Ryle (Seal)

Test: William Reamey
Henry Plear
Hannah Hatchins (her mark)

From the tone and language of this will, there was no indication whatsoever that John Ryle planned on anything other than sitting at the right hand of

The Rabbit Hash Underground Railroad Memorial, made possible by a Boone County primary education challenge grant for a legacy project. The winning students decided to use their prize money to purchase and install this bronze marker. The scope of this book did not allow for the coverage of slavery in Rabbit Hash and surrounding Boone County areas. Since Kentucky was a border state during the Civil War, with only the width of the Ohio River separating slavery from freedom, and since Boone County is bordered for nearly forty miles by this "River Jordan," there was a lot of Underground Railroad activity taking place in the area. Rising Sun itself was known to be an active station in the network. *Photo by Callie Clare.*

his God until Resurrection Day, indicating that he saw no moral or religious objection to owning slaves.

Before coming to Boone County, Kentucky, both James and John Jr. married while still living in North Carolina. As a matter of fact, they married sisters—the daughters of one of their Anson County neighbors, James Hogan and his wife Silence Hogan. James married Elizabeth Hogan, and John Jr. married Sarah (called Sallie). John Jr. sold his North Carolina lands in 1793, probably made an exploratory trip into Kentucky and then returned to North Carolina for Sarah (who was pregnant with her second child) and his daughter, Nancy. They lived in Belleview (downriver from Petersburg) for a while with his wife's brothers, who were already established in the area.

In the Boone County, Kentucky County Court Orders book (1799–1815), under Monday, December 4, 1815, it is recorded:

> *Pursuant to law the court doth establish a town upon the lands of Thomas Noble and Edward Meeks in middle creek bottom agreeably to a plott* [sic] *made and produced in court which is ordered to be recorded. Whereupon the said Noble entered into bond with John Bush and Benj G Willis his securities in the sum of Five thousand dollars conditioned pursuant to law. And thereupon Moses Scott, Jameson Hawkins*[,] *John J. Flournoy*[,] *Daniel Squires and John Brown are appointed trustees of said town which is known and called by the name Bellview* [sic] *and the said Meeks upon his part entered into bond with Cave Johnson and William Brady his Securities in the sum of $5,000 conditioned pursuant to law*[.] *This town contains about 90 acres which is vested in the above named trustees to make sale of & convey agreeably to law*[.]

This court order obviously establishes that the name Belleview was the very first name given to this area. The name Grant came into play when the magisterial districts were established, and Belleview was included in the Grant District, named for a major landowner and businessman in the town of Belleview. At that point, Belleview was often referred to as Grant, just as Rabbit Hash was referred to as Carlton.

John Jr. finally moved downriver a bit farther to Rabbit Hash, where he purchased a farm near another early family patriarch, Benjamin Stephens. John Jr. and Sarah had nine children, five boys and four girls. Two of the boys were named Whitmill and Larkin, in honor of John Jr. and James's two brothers who did not follow them to settle in Kentucky.

James and Elizabeth Ryle arrived in Boone County later, in 1795. They spent their first winter in a house at Tanner's Station, where Elizabeth gave birth to a daughter named Polly, believed to be the first white girl born in Boone County. Shortly after that, they moved to Belleview Bottoms to live with the Hogan brother there, where John Jr. and Sarah had spent some time before going to Rabbit Hash.

Herbert Ryle writes:

> *We find that in 1800 they all four joined by letter the Bullittsburg Baptist Church. In 1803 they were released by this church to constitute a Baptist Church on Woolper Creek. This church was never organized, however, and in 1803 they became charter members of the Middle Creek Baptist Church. There were twenty-three charter members. Others were Christopher Wilson, William Brady, Uriel Sebree, Jameson Hawkins, William Rogers, Elijah Hogan, Isaac Carlton, Lucy Wilson, Hetha Brady, Fanny Sebree, Ruth Hawkins, Sarah Rogers, Lucy Hogan, Nancy Carter, Mildred Sebree, Dorcas Carlton, and two colored, Anthony and Alice.*

Of the six offspring of John Ryle Sr., three (John Jr., James and Mary) left North Carolina to settle in Boone County, Kentucky; one had died while still in North Carolina (Elizabeth); and two became lost in history (Larkin and Whitmill). Mary had married Moses Scott in North Carolina before following her brothers to Kentucky. Scott was a Baptist preacher. She apparently died at an early age while in Kentucky, and she is lost from the historical record as well. She did give birth to two offspring fathered by Scott: William Scott, born around 1794, and Rebecca Scott, born around 1799. Both eventually married Ryle first cousins. Moses Scott remarried and fathered at least seven more children.

HISTORY OF THE EAST BEND NEIGHBORHOOD

Along this stretch of the Ohio River in western Boone County, Kentucky, there are the towns of Petersburg, originally Tanner's Station at Mile #493.0; Belleview, or Belleview Bottoms, at Mile #500.7 (sometimes spelled Bellevue, which confuses it with the Campbell County river town of the same name and spelling upriver at Mile #466.1); and Rabbit Hash, originally Carlton, at Mile #504.0. Right below Rabbit Hash, the Ohio River takes an almost ninety-degree bend to the left, called East Bend. There is a huge expanse of fertile bottomland here on the left bank, or Kentucky side (in river navigation terms, the banks are determined by downstream orientation, so the Kentucky bank is the left bank, and the Indiana bank is the right bank, just as the river miles are measured as the number of miles downstream from Pittsburgh, all from the downriver perspective). This large section of farmland community is known as East Bend Bottoms or, in times past, the East Bend Neighborhood. In today's vernacular, it is a suburb of Rabbit Hash, and it includes the drainages of Sparks Branch (Mile 504.0), Little Ranty Creek (Mile 505.3), Big Ranty Creek (Mile 505.6), De Hart Run (Mile 506.7), Lick Creek (Mile 509.6), Gunpowder Creek (Mile 511.2) and Landing Creek (Little Gunpowder; Mile 512.3).

In the late eighteenth and early nineteenth centuries, some prestigious, if not famous, family names were associated with the East Bend Neighborhood. In 1782, Humphrey Marshall came to this part of Kentucky as the official Fayette County surveyor (Boone County was not established as a county until 1798), and he had a land grant for four thousand acres, which he exercised and thereby acquired land in East Bend. Humphrey Marshall was raised and educated in Virginia with his cousin John (who would later serve as chief justice of the United States Supreme Court longer than any other chief justice). Humphrey eventually owned more land than any other Kentuckian at that date, as he continued in his business of real estate and landholding by acquiring land warrants and military grants from others. He is most remembered in Kentucky history as the author of *The History of Kentucky* in 1812. The book contained very stinging and biased editorial political overtones. He was also the man who, while serving in the Kentucky legislature in 1808–9, challenged and fought Henry Clay in a duel. Since dueling was outlawed in Kentucky, they had to go to Indiana Territory to carry out the meeting. After firing three separate volleys, both men were wounded but survived, and the duel was declared over by their seconds.

That same year, Humphrey Marshall sold his East Bend property to Thomas Carneal, whose son, Thomas D. Carneal (a partner in the Covington Company, which acquired land in northern Kentucky and later founded and laid out the city of Covington), would eventually sell it to Robert Piatt, who eventually built his plantation estate, Winfield Cottage, there and established Piatt's Landing and Ferry. There was even an official post office there from 1833 to 1848 called Piatt's Landing Post Office. Winfield Cottage was a unique mansion-villa oriented to the river. Its high-style architecture was most unusual for this area of the country. It was a well-known landmark up and down the Ohio River well into the twentieth century. Its name was not given by Robert but by a later owner. Robert Piatt was a member of the Piatt family out of New

The Piatt's Landing, Kentucky historical marker. *Photo by Callie Clare. Courtesy of the Rabbit Hash Historical Society.*

Jersey whose brothers all served as officers in the Revolutionary War and who eventually used their land grants to claim property both in northern Kentucky at North Bend and East Bend and in Ohio. They became an influential family in the mercantile, banking and law professions in Cincinnati.

Dr. Israel T. Canby established himself in Boone County about the same time as Robert Piatt. They became neighbors, and their families intermingled. Dr. Canby and Elizabeth Piatt (daughter of Robert) married, and on November 9, 1817, a son, Edward Richard Sprigg Canby, was born. E.R.S. Canby was destined for a military career and to become a military hero, making the ultimate sacrifice for his country. He graduated West Point in 1839 at age twenty-two and subsequently

> *served in the Florida War, Mexican War, Frontier Duty in Utah and New Mexico, was severely wounded at White River in Arkansas during the Civil War but later accepted the final surrender of Confederate forces from General Richard Taylor (son of Zachary Taylor) at Critronelle, Alabama on May 4, 1865 and from General Kirby Smith at New Orleans on May 26, 1885…General Canby as he became known was sent to northern California to arrange a conference with Modoc Indians and was slain by "Captain Jack" their leader on April 18, 1873.*

Historically, East Bend has always depended on agriculture and river commerce for its subsistence. Piatt's Landing, Piatt's Ferry across the river to North's Landing and Kirtley Landing at the mouth of Lick Creek were

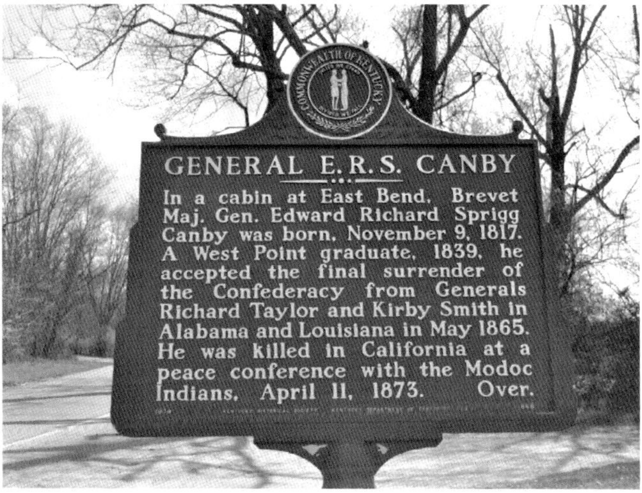

The General E.R.S. Canby Kentucky historical marker. *Photo by Callie Clare. Courtesy of the Rabbit Hash Historical Society.*

all charted steamboat landings on early river charts and maps along the east bend of the Ohio River. The rich bottomlands of Upper and Lower East Bend Bottoms to this day produce some of the highest-quality agricultural produce found in Boone County. Except for the East Bend Power Generating Station, this area remains solely agricultural, some land being farmed by the same family names from generations past.

East Bend has no commercial center other than Rabbit Hash. But it does lay claim to housing two proportionally large congregation places of worship, the East Bend Baptist Church established in 1819 and the East Bend Methodist Episcopal Church established in the late 1850s. Perhaps there is truth to the claim that the yeoman is God's chosen one.

In 1876, there appeared in the *Rising Sun Register* of Ohio County, Indiana, a three-part series entitled simply "History of the East Bend Neighborhood." This is a rare and valuable secondary resource simply because of the sheer paucity of extant written or recorded historical information available concerning the early history of these communities, most of which would disappear in recurring floods set on obliterating all evidence of former human occupation on the flood plain. There is enough evidence to suggest that this series of articles was penned by William H. Nelson of Rabbit Hash. One of his documented occupations was that of newspaperman, both in Lawrenceburg and in Rising Sun, Indiana. There is also a Nelson connection in both the Ryle and Stephens families, which could account for the specific Ryle/Stephens references in the interview. It is included here just as it appeared in the Indiana city's newsprint:

August 4, 1876—Washington Irving said: "What has been the fate of many of the fair cities of antiquity, whose numberless ruins encumber the plains of Europe and Asia, and awaken the fruitless inquiry of the traveler? They have sunk into dust and silence, they have perished from remembrance for want of an historian!" [From *A History of New York, From the Beginning of the World to the End of the Dutch Dynasty*, by Diedrich Knickerbocker (Washington Irving; London, 1820).]

To rescue from oblivion that portion of Boone County known as "East Bend Neighborhood" will be the object of this and following sketches, and in order that the reader may more fully understand and comprehend this history, he is asked to allow his mind to run back in imagination to the times of which these sketches treat; to the time when there was not even the sign of a habitation, except at long intervals along the Ohio River; when there were but a log hut or two where the beautiful little city of Rising Sun now stands, to the time when the half dozen families only that were in the neighborhood, lived in little cabins with stick chimneys or floors of any kind; to the time when wolves, bears, and other wild animals infested the country; when the cooking, eating, and sleeping were done in one small room, and to the time when if a family left one portion of the country to settle in another, there was no going back, and very little or nothing heard from the ones left behind.

The earliest recollection of this neighborhood that is known, or ever will be known, dates from the 6th of March, 1806, the day on which Benjamin Stephens settled on the Ohio River, just below the mouth of Bank Lick Creek [now Lick Creek], *on the farm now owned by Omar Kirtly. This being the case, a sketch of his earlier life in connection with what is known about the few who were here prior to him, will necessarily be first in this history.*

Benjamin Stephens was born in Orange County, Virginia May 30, 1779. When 20 years of age, or in 1799, he was married to Miss Agnes Nelson, who was born in the same county, February 6, 1782. Their first child, James Nelson, now living in the neighborhood, was born March 11, 1800, and their second, William Robinson, died some years since, was born October 16, 1802. Shortly after this last event they removed to South Carolina, where they remained for about two years, after which they came to Harrison County, Kentucky, where they lived until they started for Boone County. Benjamin Stephens inherited his father's given name, which he transmitted to one of his sons and numerous grand, great, and great- great grand sons. His father had no brothers or sisters, but Benjamin had six brothers and two sisters—Waller, Richard, William, John, Leonard and

Edmond, and Nancy Sandford and Polly Herndon. Waller died in South Carolina, Richard in Alabama, and William in Monroe County, Missouri. The rest, including the father, came to Northern Kentucky and settled in what is now known as Kenton and Boone Counties, where they all lived and where they all have died, with the exception of Mrs. Sandford, who is still living with her children in and about Covington. Benjamin's brother, William, came with him to the neighborhood where they farmed together one year, after which William went to Kenton County. William's family consisted of his wife, who was a sister of Benjamin's wife, and one child. Benjamin's family consisted of the two children already named, and an adopted girl, Milly, aged 12 years, who was given to them by Mrs. Stephens, who is now living in Rising Sun, and of whom we shall occasion to speak again of hereafter.

When the family came here they found perhaps a half dozen other families scattered along the river and Gun Powder Creek. The day they came a man named Keenean vacated the house into which they moved and went across the creek near which place a man lived named Shackleford. Further up the river on the farm now owned by a man named Carneal, lived a family of negroes. The next and only settlement on the river was that of John Neal, who lived just below the mouth of DeHart Creek, on the farm now owned by James Hastings, the house standing on the river bank opposite where Mr. Hastings's residence now stands.

Mr. Neal had five sons—Benjamin, Matthew, William, John, and Thomas, and three daughters—Betsy, Sallie, and Annie. Benjamin died in Ohio, and Matthew it is supposed in Montgomery County, Kentucky, and John in Iowa. Sallie married a man named Shackelford, and died in Ohio. Betsy married a Hodges, and Annie's first husband was Archibald Ruddle, father of Theodore Ruddle of Rising Sun. Her second husband was named Baas. She died in Arkansas. Thomas died in Rising Sun and William and Betsy in East Bend.

The exact date at which John Neal came isn't known, but it was about the year 1801. There appears to have been quite a number of John Neals, and each one had some qualifying appellation to distinguish him from the others. The old gentleman was always known as "Grandfather John." He had a grandson who was a blacksmith and was called "Smith John." Grandfather John's son was known as Hessian John. There was a nephew that went by the name of "Big John." He also had two other grandsons named John, but their distinguishing adjectives do not appear to have been remembered.

There had been another settlement just about the mouth of DeHart Creek by a man named DeHart, from which the Creek took its name, but he was gone when John Neal came, and the general supposition was that he had been killed by Indians. He lived then alone, having no family, and there is a tradition that he had a large sum of money, in silver, which he kept in a little bag, and that at some time prior to his death he had hid it in the hollow of some of the old Sycamore trees that were standing along the banks of the creek. The mysterious "jack-o'lanterns" [sound familiar?] *were frequently seen along this creek, and some of the inhabitants explained the phenomenon by saying it was the reflection of Old DeHart's silver.*

The nearest settlement was on Gun Powder Creek where it is crossed by the Rabbit Hash and Big Bone road, a man named John Click living there. The next and last was about a mile or so farther up the creek, where Reuben Searcy lived, it being the farm now occupied by James Aylor.

The families living at Bellevue were the Ryles, who came from North Carolina, the Howletts, and Hogans. The two Ryle boys, John and James, came to the county two years before the Stephens family, and stopped for a while in Tanner's Fort at Petersburg, the remains of which are still visible. John Ryle had four sons and four daughters. Their names being John, Whitmill, Larkin and Sandy, and Nancy, Sall, Polly and Betsy. Nancy married Francis Craig, Sally married Jarrett Kendall, Polly, Lewis Willis, and Betsy was the first wife of J. W. Pearson of Rising Sun. James Ryle had seven sons and one daughter. There names were William, Larkin, James, Elijah, David, Hogan, John, and Mary, who married William Scott. David Ryle married Elizabeth Hayden Stephens, the eldest daughter of Benjamin Stephens. He outlived all his brothers and sisters, and was, prior to his death, which occurred in 1875, the oldest man living who was born in the county. William Scott was about the year 1819 thrown from a young horse and almost instantly killed.

The day on which the Stephens boys arrived at East Bend the peach trees were in full bloom, and it is further remembered that they were killed by frost late in May. They suffered considerably from sickness being caused by several large swampy lakes in the bottoms near them. The chills got such a deep hold on them that it was fully five years before they got entirely rid of the malaria. The first bear seen by them was a half-grown one that the Ryle boys chased down from Bellevue, and had killed near the mouth of Gunpowder Creek, and one of them was carrying it before him on a horse. Several other bears were seen afterward, but the settlers were not troubled a great deal by them.

The marketing in those days, and for many years afterwards, was all put in a pirogue—a little canoe, formed from the trunk of a tree, and rowed and cordelled all the way to Cincinnati, which place then consisted of a few log cabins and roughly constructed frame houses. In those days there was a great deal of honey found in the woods, and it was one of the chief articles marketed, it being roughly sold at 25cts a pound. They had plenty of fish and other game in those early days. The fish were caught by means of a gig from a canoe. In the days before steamboats or other artificial disturbances of the water, the fish floated along near the surface and close to the shore, and thus it was no trouble to catch all one wanted.

The only mill in the whole section was Garnett's, on the same site as which it now stands, and where the farmers have gotten pretty much all their corn ground from that day to present.

There were a few settlers at Big Bone at this time, and considerable salt was made from the water of the springs which have since become so famous, but this was abandoned after a few years as unprofitable, on account of the great quantity of water required to produce a little salt. It appears that there was a great demand for salt, at a high price, and when a batch was made there was always a customer ready to take it off the dry-board before the water had drained out.

A joke is told on Mr. Stephens in connection with this salt business. He went for a sack of salt one day, and there being none dry he had his sack filled with the wet salt, threw it on his horse and started for home, to find out when he got there the brine had run out over the horse and taken nearly all the hair off.

August, 18, 1876—The only persons now remembered living at Big Bone at that time [1806] *were Charles O'Neal, father of John O'Neal, now living in East Bend Bottoms, Zella Miss and Samuel Glore. Mr. Glore worked at the blacksmith and cabinet trades. Mr. J.N. Stephens now has in his possession a table and chest of black walnut, made by Mr. Glore over seventy years ago. They have been in constant use ever since they were made, and still they are as good, almost, as new.*

Mr. Glore had the only grindstone in the whole country around, and people were known to go eight or ten miles to get their axes ground. When Mr. Stephens came from South Carolina, to Harrison County, Kentucky, besides the ones who came to East Bend were his father and youngest brother, Leonard, who went to South Carolina to bring them out. "Aunt Milly" (a colored woman in the family) relates several anectdotes [sic] *and incidents that occurred on the way. She seems to have a very good remembrance of things that happened then. When being questioned as to whether or not she remembered when she came to East Bend, she replied, "Lawsee, I'se done forgot things that happened that summer, but all dem things I remembers just as well as if they happened yesterday." They started with a lot of cattle, two horses and a wagon, their tent and cooking utensils, which were few. They had to sell their wagon at Cumberland Gap, and make the rest of the journey in a one horse cart, one or the other of them riding the extra horse. She remembers them making a long march one day to get to a good pond of water, and which was known to them as a good place to rest for a day or two. They got there after dark, pitched their tents, cooked and ate their suppers and the next morning found out the water they used was "dipped up from the side of an old dead horse that had been in the water for some days," and which they had supposed in the darkness was a log.*

William, who was then only about four years of age, did not have much affection for any of them except Milly, who was then about eleven or twelve years old, and when any of them requested the pleasure of his company to travel with them, he always rebelled, and manifested this rebellion by yelling vociferiously [sic]. *He was finally told by his grandfather that if he would be a good boy and not cry any more until he got to Kentucky, he would buy him a blue cradle and a goat* [the term cradle in this instance probably referred to a small wooden device in which to carry things, like a small goat cart]. *The distance they had to go, and the speed at which they had to travel were wearisome to the strongest, and to a child it was exceedingly so. So William soon got so that he not only wanted to travel with Milly but he cried lustily for hours for his "boo tradle and yote" as he called them. His grandfather having tried to appease his desires and quiet his yelling by "moral swasion" then resorted to the sterner method of corporal punishment, and the way, as she says, "He turned up that boy's dress and painted him with the flat of his hand," was a caution for him to never cry for his blue cradle and goat during the rest of the journey.*

The day that they arrived at Lexington was a very cold one, and Milly for the first time in her life saw a stove. They all went in to warm and there was a crowd of men standing around in a certain corner, but she, as soon as she saw there was no fire in the room, stopped at the door, saying it was about as warm out of doors as it was in the house without any fire. They insisted on her going up to the corner and finally she consented, and says that she noticed that she felt warmer, but still she couldn't see no fire, until someone opened the stove door and explained it to her. The first stove she had ever seen or did see for a long while afterward, and here it might be added, that as long as Mr. Stephens lived he never used a stove either for cooking or heating. The cooking was always done in a large fireplace six or eight feet square supplied with a crane, or as it was called in olden times "potracks," and skillets, griddles, split-jacks, etc. Corn bread was often cooked on a board, and to roast a turkey they would hang it up by a string before the fire and it would turn round and round. This method of cooking was pursued by his family, and by his oldest son, James, until about the close of the war, or until the negroes left. This was not done, however, as a matter of economy, by any means, but because they considered the cooking better, and it really was better than stove cooking; and who is there in the neighborhood now, past the age of maturity, that has not eaten and enjoyed the splendid and many large dinners cooked in this way at his residence?

The trip from Harrison County to East Bend, though not so long a one, was attended with many difficulties, the principal one being that there was no road the greater part of the way, and they could only find their way by the blazed trees; that is, the trees had the bark cut off on one side to show the direction to travel. When they arrived at East Bend they had two horses and a cart, two cows and calves and two yearling steers, and though, as "Aunt Milly" now says, they were as "poor as dogs," they were rich in comparison to others who lived in the neighborhood.

In just eight days after their arrival Richard was born, it being March 14. 1806. "Aunt Milly" was asked, in order to find out if her memory was as correct as she thought it to be, if she was sure that he was born while they lived on the river? "What, dat chile? I guess I is sure. I don't know the day of the week. Nor de year but dat very Mars Dick Stephens was born on the river, in about a week after we come. Didn't have no doctor in dem days, neither. He growed to be a big fine looking man, but he was the littlest, puniest baby ever born. His head wasn't no bigger'n my fists and before he was a year old he came near dying with the "bull hives" [the term hives was also used to mean the croup, laryngitis and rattles, indicating an upper respiratory condition]. *It seems strange how they could get along without doctors those days, when they seem to be so absolutely necessary now, and are notified some time previous to those—well—those "events that cast their shadows before them."*

Mr. Stephens was considered a very good doctor by the inhabitants of the neighborhood, and he was often sent for. The only treatment in those days were bleeding and pills made from the boiled juice of walnut bark.

While they lived on the river, his father immigrated from Virginia and settled in Kenton County, on what is now known as the Leonard Stephens' farm, where he lived and died. He came down to see them once, and brought behind him on his horse, "Jordan," a little negro boy about six years old, and gave him to them. Another child, Lucy Nelson, was born while they lived there, but she only lived a few months. She was born February 6, 1808.

The following reminiscences of the John Neal family was written by Theodore Ruddell of this city, who is a grandson of Mr. Neal.

John Neal, Sr., moved on the farm now owned and occupied by James Hastings about the year 1801, as near as the writer can fix the date, as all the family is now dead. He paid for his land three times. Who the first two were that received the pay I do not know, but the last was David Carneal. His upper line was on the river and was Andrew Dolph's upper line. His lower line is James Hastings' lower line. The back line was a straight line with Hastings' back line. Mr. Neal's wife's name was Agnes; his children's names were William, Elizabeth, Benjamin, Matthew, John, Sally, Thomas and Annie. He had a brother, Moses, who also came to the "Bend," but was dead before this writer can remember. The family was full of Johns, as has already been mentioned. Mr. Neal first built a house of round logs, of but one room, which was his residence until his youngest child was married, when it was exchanged for a house of hewed logs. With the boys he soon cleared and fenced what was long known "Grand Daddy Neal's Big Field." It hardly deserves the name as it was said to contain 16 acres, but I don't believe there were more than 12. Mr. Neal set out quite a respectable orchard of good apples, which were cut down several years ago, being too old to be profitable. He gave farms to four of his children off of his land and left the home farm to his youngest. Two of his children raised large families and died on their land. These were William and Elizabeth. The rest sold and left the country to go farther west, and but few of Mr. Neal's descendants are now living in East Bend. There also came to the neighborhood a relative of his named Mitchell, who cleared an acre or so of land, which became famous for "possum fruit," having grown up in paw paw bushes. All the boys for a long time knew where to find "Mitchell's Clearing," and many a gray head remembers how he gorged his stomach on the fruit that grew in that renowned boy's paradise. It is now a very small part of Solon Stephens' farm. John Neal and his wife were both born in the colony of Virginia, of parents from Ireland who were sold to the bidder of the lowest number of years to pay their passage from the old country. John Neal died March, 1831, aged 85 years and 5 days. Agnes Neal, whose maiden name was Fisher, lived until April, 1847, and died, I think, in the 98th year of her age. Most of this was told the writer by his mother, who was a child of four years when the family moved to the place, and a great deal he recollects himself.

After John Neal had cleared his big field, one day some of the family saw a bear standing at the head of the field, on the bank of the river, and Frank, the black man, was sent to shoot it, which he did, giving it a death wound, but it didn't die immediately. It started down the river bank toward the house, and Mr. Neal went out to stop it, without even his cane. Thomas was sent to let go the dog which was tied, but the dog cut up so he couldn't get the rope from his neck, and he finally had to untie the other end and let the dog drag it after him. In the meantime the bear was coming very close to Mr. Neal, showing him a dangerous set of "ivories," with the determination to use them, and Mr. Neal was squaring himself off for a vigorous kick at his bearship. Frank was coming, but a good piece off, and had the gun by the barrel with the breech raised above his head intending to use it for a club. Just then "Trim" was lossed [sic], *and before the bear knew it the dog had him by the "breeches," and had jerked him down the bank. The bear, thus taken by surprise, tried to spring up a tree, but the canine caught him and pulled him down. Bruin tried it two or three times but finally gave it up, turning his back to the tree and assuming a defensive position and knocking the dog off when he came too close, and forcing him to keep a respectable distance. Frank now came up and commenced loading his gun, but it was not necessary for poor Bruin soon fell over dead. Well that dog was like some of the orthodox Christians. He believed in punishment after death, for the way he did shake that bear showed that he meant to punish him even if he were dead. Fearing he would spoil the meat and hide he was taken off. The bear fought well for he was fighting for life, liberty, and the pursuit of happiness; but bearsteak was in order that evening for supper. The writer has heard the parties tell of that fight at least a dozen times.*

September 15, 1876—Benjamin Stephens moved in August, 1808, from his farm in East Bend to the farm on the hill which has been known for a long time as the "Old Place." Here he lived until the time of his death, and here all of his children were born who have not already been mentioned.

Geographically speaking, the farm lies on the North side of Gunpowder creek about three miles from its mouth, and extending over toward the Ohio River, containing 217 acres, for which he paid $3.50 per acre. When he first came to the place he built a log hut just below the old spring so familiar to everybody, and where the Rabbit Hash and Union graded road now lies, being near the road. This was the first settlement on the hills nearer Burlington [the county seat]. *The land here as well as everywhere else was covered with heavy timber and it was with no little difficulty that it*

A family photograph of Benjamin Haydon Stephens and his wife and children. Benjamin's sister Jane Kendall Stephens married James A. Wilson, the first proprietor of the Rabbit Hash General Store. Their grandfather, Benjamin Stephens Jr., was the patriarch of the Stephens family in Boone County, Kentucky. *From left to right, standing*: Connie (Stephens) Rouse, Edna Bettie (Stephens) Allen, Harry Stephens, Nannie M. (Stephens) Stephens (married another Stephens), Lucy H. (Stephens) Ryle. *Seated*: James [*sic*] Mary (Mason) Stephens and Benjamin Haydon Stephens. They married on February 20, 1862. *From author's personal collection.*

was cleared. Leases were generally taken from four to six years, and Mr. Stephens leased his farm, or rather, tract, for six years. It was a rule that all trees measuring under eighteen inches in diameter were to be cut down, trees larger than that they "deadened." His first lease was from Humphrey Marshall. At the end of six years John Guy Marshall had control of the land by some means, and although all the land in the neighborhood was selling at two dollars per acre, he was required to pay a dollar and a half per acre more for the improvements he had put upon it. It may seem a little strange to some that he would leave the bottoms to come up on the hill, when he could have gotten that land just as cheap, but it was on account of the continual chills and fever down there. Only a single case of ague can now be remembered to have been contracted on the "Old Place."

The next house built was the one that is yet standing. It is very pleasantly situated, about two hundred yards this side of the Gunpowder Ridge, and had it been built at a later day it would undoubtedly have been built on the ridge, but in primitive times they had to build without regard to beauty of location, but the convenience of the spring. The old black-heart cherry that now stands on the road, on T.C.S. Ryle's farm was probably the first fruit tree of any kind ever planted in the neighborhood. It was the first in the hills, at least. Shortly after Mr. Stephens moved to this place, within a month or two, James Ryle moved from Bellevue, to his old place, where his son, Hogan, lived and died. This is about one mile from the Stephens farm. Soon after this John Ryle moved from Bellevue out to the farm now occupied by Mrs. Harriett Walton, on the East Bend and Burlington road, about two miles from Rabbit Hash, it being also about a mile and a half from where his brother James settled.

These settlements, with the ones mentioned before, on the river and Gunpowder, were the only ones for several years. The next settlements were made on the hill by Joseph Graves, who lived on the farm owned by David Ryle, lately deceased, which is about one mile lower down the Gunpowder Ridge, and Philip Graves his brother, who settled on the hill part of the Omar Kirtly [sic] *farm.*

While it is the case, that these early settlers had a great deal of difficulties to contend with, they had a great deal of enjoyment. They were away from relatives and friends, it's true, but their health was good and they had many luxuries in the way of eating, at least, that we do not have now. Wild turkeys abounded in great numbers, and ten or fifteen were often caught at one time in a coop or rail pens.

They were always fat and fine, and some times when they were shot from the tall trees, in falling to the ground they would burst. When a great many were caught they were salted down for winter use or taken to Cincinnati and sold. Deer were also very plentiful and they would often come right up to the door. Hogs were one of the principal products in those days and they have continued so to the present. It cost nothing to fatten them, as there was always plenty of mast. The only trouble was keeping them tame. They had to run at large in the woods, of course, and when killing time came they had to go out and find them and kill them one at a time, where ever they happened to be. The pigs when very young were all caught and marked after the style which now prevails in order to distinguish them. Mr. Stephens' *mark was a slit in each ear and a shallow fork in the right. This mark he used as long as he lived. Sheep were raised tolerably early, but the wool made them a great deal of trouble to take care of. A flock would sometimes wander a great distance from the house, and would often be chased to the cabin in broad day light. They used bells a great deal in those days and when the flock would come with a great rush toward the house with bells all jingling they well knew the wolves were after them. Corn was the first of the cereal products to be raised. Wheat soon became to be raised to a small extent, but it was sometimes the case that it would become diseased in some way, and it made everybody "Wheat-sick," who ate it. The first pork ever sold in the neighborhood brought about two and a half cents, and it continued at that price for a long time. Milk cows were worth from about $6.00 to $10.00; and for many years a bushel of wheat would just buy a bushel of salt.*

Elizabeth was the first child born to Mr. and Mrs. Stephens after moving to the old place. She was born April 19, 1809, and was married to David Ryle January 15, 1824, in the fifteenth year of her age. The cabin that was built on coming to the hill, was one of two rooms. The logs were put up just as they were cut from the tree, but were afterwards blazed a little on the inside, and the cracks stopped with mud. The floors were made of puncheon, and doors they had none. In cold weather they would set up a few puncheons, in front of it, or hang some kind of covering over it. This served them for a great many years until they built the one that now marks the old place.

Grinding corn on a hand mill was very slow work, and the idea of a horse mill was early conceived and put in execution. The first mill was built on the ridge, north of the graveyard, and not far from where the old barn stood. The motive power for this was horses, which pulled by a shaft. Another mill run in the same manner was afterward put up near the first one, and long after was erected the old tread mill, the remains of which are now to be seen. This was for a long time considered to be the best mill in the country, making both meal and bolted flour. The milling previous to this was done either at South Fork, or at Garnett Mill on Middle Greek. "Aunt Milly" now tells how she used to go up there, a distance of about eight or ten miles, all alone on horseback with a grist, and no road or anything to guide her, save the blazed trees. She also tells how they went to church at Middle Creek in those days. Mr. and Mrs. Stephens had horses and could ride, but she would often walk the entire distance. The Ryles and many others who afterward moved to the neighborhood, would take their shoes and stockings in their hands and carry them until they came to a spring near the church, where they would all stop, wash their feet, put on their shoes and stockings and go in. This was done as a matter of economy to save their shoes, both by the young men and young ladies and while in each other's company.

The first school house that was built, was in the year 1810 or 1811, on the farm now owned by Mrs. J.C. McConnell, near the East Bend and Big Bone road, on the grounds where the North Bend Baptist Association was held for many years. It was the rudest kind of a structure possible to imagine. It was very small, and was made of plain round logs with a large fire place and a quinquangular [sic] *chimney. A portion of a log was cut out on two sides for a window, and for glass they used paper, greased. The first man to have ever taught the young ideas other than how to shoot was William Hodges, who married a daughter of John Neal, already mentioned. He was the father of the late William Hodges, who so many of the citizens now living in the neighborhood remember, and the grandfather of the several Hodges boys now living in the East Bend.*

Although he never lived in the immediate neighborhood, its history would be incomplete without a mention of Mr. Robert Mosby, well known to all the residents here. He was born on the 25th of December, 1786, in Bourbon County, Kentucky. His father having settled there in 1780. They moved to Boone County, and he has lived during his entire life within three miles of his present home on the hill between Woolper Creek and Petersburg. He was married in the year 1814—about the time of which the above articles treat—to Spangler, of Petersburg. They lived together for half a century until the year 1864, when Mrs. Mosby died in the joyful anticipation of a brighter and holier existence in the abode of eternal felicity. Notwithstanding Mr. Mosby has the weight of these many years upon his shoulders, yet his form is erect and step firmer than most men who have reached three score and ten. His mental faculties remain good, and he is able to relate many scenes of early life in the "dark and bloody ground." His father was intimately acquainted with Daniel Boone and his contemporary frontiersmen. If he lives until the 25th of December, he will be ninety years of age.

The author of the above articles apparently felt compelled to add that final paragraph in order to lend some credence and pride to the importance that the early history of the Rabbit Hash/East Bend area has in the overall history of Boone County. By including the fact that Mr. Mosby's father was an intimate friend of Daniel Boone certainly justifies the use of the newspaper space dedicated to the neighborhood, not only across the river from Rising Sun, but also in an altogether different state. But realistically, being across the river from Rabbit Hash back in 1876 was really not that much different from being across the street in any other community. The river was not the overwhelmingly restrictive barrier back then as it is nowadays. People regularly crossed back and forth on a daily basis with not much trouble or effort at all. The ferry was as easy and convenient as walking over a bridge, and in times of ice or low-water level, they simply walked across. Relatives and friends lived on both sides of the river, and they communicated with one another on a regular basis. Rabbit Hash folks attended school and church in Rising Sun. They frequented the various merchants and professionals there for goods and services. They even went across the river to be embalmed and buried. Both sides of the river sported physicians' offices, and people from Rising Sun came to Rabbit Hash for their "doctoring" needs and vice versa. It wasn't until the navigational improvements on the river system that raised the pool level and provided for year-round navigation began to appear that physical communication between the two towns began to suffer, and then when the ferry quit running in 1945, that communication ceased altogether. Now it takes an hour or more to drive over to Rising Sun unless one owns his own water craft. Today, it really is like traveling to another state.

THE STEPHENS FAMILY

As reported in the aforementioned newspaper series published in the *Rising Sun Register*, the first of the Stephens family to settle in the Rabbit Hash/East Bend area was Benjamin Stephens Jr. He was the second-born child of Benjamin Stephens and Dorothy Jemima Waller Stephens:

> *They had nine children who lived to adulthood. All were born in Orange County, Virginia. Sometime after October 25, 1805, Benjamin and Dorothy and most of their children moved to near Bryant's Station in Kentucky. About after two years, Benjamin, Sr., Benjamin, Jr., William, Leonard, and John moved by the Ridge Road north to the Ohio River. Benjamin, Jr. and William settled in what is now Boone County.*

The others wound up in Kenton and Campbell Counties.

In 1799, while still in Virginia, Benjamin Jr. married Agnes Nelson, the daughter of James Nelson and Lucy Robinson. (Lucy's sister Agnes married

Benjamin Jr.'s older brother, Edmund.) It is believed that Benjamin Jr. and Agnes moved to South Carolina with Edmund and Agnes in 1802. It was sometime after 1805 that they finally settled in East Bend on Gunpowder Creek. Together, they had fourteen children, only two of whom died in infancy. Brother William had married Elizabeth Louise Nelson back in Virginia. She was a sister of Agnes Nelson. After remaining in Boone County for a few years with Ben and Agnes, they moved in 1810 to Monroe County, Missouri, where they purchased a large farm.

According to Herbert E. Ryle in the Stephens/Ryle book, there is a paucity of information available about the ancestry of Benjamin Sr.'s mother and father, except for her name and her parents. He writes:

> *Blessing Stephens, who married Stephen Smith on July 4, 1773, was the daughter of William Stephens whose will was recorded in Orange County in 1767. On July 3, 1773 Blessing and Stephen entered into an agreement whereby each agrees to respect the other's property and to manage and dispose of it as each saw fit. The agreement presents a picture of two mature individuals entering into an equal contract. Stephen, at that time was a 58 year old widower with five married daughters and extensive property, and Blessing was in her late thirties, with a nineteen year old son, Benjamin…* [who] *could well have been the illegitimate son of these two, or he could have been the son of Blessing and a Stephens cousin. There were other Stephens in Orange County and adjoining Spotsylvania County. After General Braddock's defeat in 1754, General Washington noted in his journal that "a Capt. William Stephens had been left with the wounded." He is not mentioned again. Blessing could have been a widow at a very early age, and Benjamin may even have been a posthumous child. This conjecture seems to be more likely, because years later, Milly, an ex-slave of the Stephens family and a great granddaughter of Benjamin Stephens who lived in Missouri, both said, "Old Benjamin Stephens had no brothers or sisters." Although Stephen Smith in his 1799 will several times refers to Benjamin Stephens as "my son," if he really were his son he would have had at least five half sisters and possibly two half brothers. This would have hardly been overlooked by later family members. It is more likely that Stephen Smith formed a close attachment to the nineteen year old son of the young woman he married, and having no sons of his own living with him, he grew to look upon him as a son. Benjamin's son, Leonard, in his 1855 diary of his visit to his old home, refers to "Aunt Stewart's spring," so there is evidence that the children of Benjamin Stephens called the five daughters*

of Stephen Smith "Aunt." But whatever the relationship was between Benjamin Stephens, Blessing Stephens, and Stephen Smith, Stephen, in his 1799 will, made him co-equal with his five daughters in sharing his estate and named him whole and sole executor of his will…

After their marriage in 1775 Benjamin Stephens [Sr.] *and Dorothy Waller evidently settled in next to Stephen Smith's home on the hill overlooking the Riga, about one mile north of Orange Springs. However, during the fall and winter of 1777–78 Benjamin was part of the guard assigned to protect the commissioners from Virginia and North Carolina who were appointed to run the boundary line west to the Mississippi. This line is the present day boundary between Kentucky and Tennessee. That was a very cold winter, and one chronicler wrote that rivers and streams froze up that were never before frozen in the memories of men. Somewhere west of the Cumberland Mountains a disagreement broke out between the two sides of the party and the Commissioners and guard from North Carolina went back home. Some of the fifty man guard from Virginia then demanded to be allowed to return home and all but eight left. Those eight and the Virginia Commissioners finished the job. We don't know which group Benjamin Stephens* [Sr.] *was in.*

During the two tumultuous decades which followed the Revolution approximately one third of the population of Virginia moved West of the Appalachians to the new states of Kentucky and Tennessee. The Benjamin Stephens family of Orange County finally made the move in October 1805, later than some, but still earlier than most. Benjamin, then fifty-one years old, filed the final Court papers as administrator of the estate of Stephen Smith on October 5, 1805. On October 6th he and Dorothy sold their 631½ acre plantation on the Riga…We don't know why they waited until then until deciding to move, but it could have been that Blessing died that year. Benjamin reported that the widow received her annual legacy of five barrels of corn in 1804, but after that she is not mentioned. Family history does not include mention of his mother accompanying the family to Kentucky, and her grave site has not been identified in Kentucky.

There is evidence that three sons, Waller, Edmund and Benjamin, Jr. had left Orange County earlier and moved with their families to South Carolina. Dorothy's brother, John Waller, had moved to Abbeville, South Carolina earlier and it is possible these young men went there to join their uncle. In 1876, ex-slave Millie, in her contribution to the history of the Stephens family, says that the ones in South Carolina got into serious trouble and old Benjamin and his youngest son, Leonard, had to go down and

> *bring them out. Just what the trouble was is not stated, but we do know that Agnes Robinson Stephens, wife of Edmund Stephens, died in South Carolina, and it appears that Waller Stephens died or disappeared about the same time. It could be that the trouble was sickness or Indian trouble.*
>
> *Virginia pioneers moving to Kentucky traveled south to North Carolina along what was known as the Great National Road. Travel was relatively easy with wagons, carriages and horse or ox teams carrying most of the possessions. Most of the men rode horseback. When they reached the Cumberland Gap, however, things were different. Daniel Boone's Wilderness Trace was not wide enough or good enough to admit wagons. Therefore all possessions had to be re-packed and only the most valuable or most necessary were kept. These were stowed in packs or in narrow two-wheeled carts. Cattle, sheep, horses, pigs and other animals were herded along the way. The trip from the gap to Boonesborough required about a month, if the weather was good and if the Indians were not on the warpath.*
>
> *By 1805 Kentucky had been a state for thirteen years, and its population numbered more than one hundred thousand. New settlers found all the choice lands around Boonesborough taken up and had to look farther north and west to find available land to settle on. Benjamin Stephens and his family spent some time, maybe as much as two years in Fayette County. Here, the youngest son, Leonard, married Katherine Sandford, and the youngest daughter Nancy Waller Stephens, married Thomas Sandford. These Sandfords were also from Orange County, but I do not know whether they preceded or accompanied the Stephens to Kentucky.*
>
> *The Stephens family must have spent some of their time in Fayette County scouting for land on which to make their permanent homes. In 1806, Benjamin Jr. and William, and Agnes and Louise, their wives moved up north to the recently formed county of Boone.*

At this point in Herbert Ryle's book, the remainder of the history of the Stephenses' settlement in Boone County very closely mirrors the *Register* newspaper articles. He does conclude, however, with this final paragraph:

> *Benjamin Stephens, Jr. did not live to see the divisions in his family created by the Civil War. He died in 1855 at age seventy-seven…Ryles and Stephens fought for both sides. Since both families had been slave holders for at least one hundred years, there was a strong tendency for their affections to go toward the South, but both Kentucky and Missouri were Border States, and the Government exerted great efforts to keep both in the Northern camp…* [Benjamin Jr.] *left*

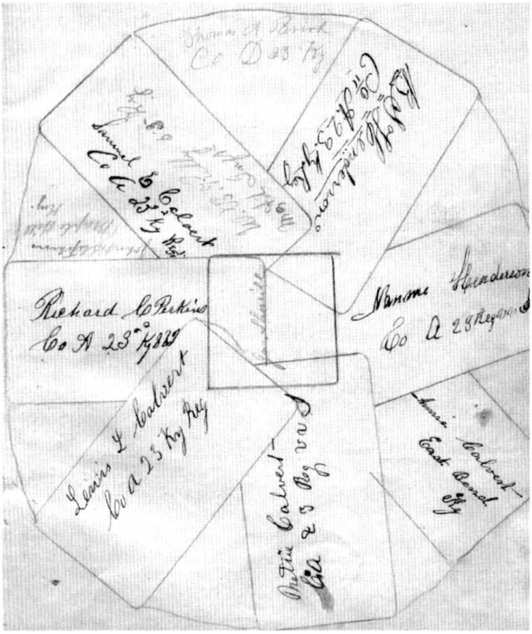

A page from the "Album of Remembrance" book belonging to Miss Pamelia Stephens of Rabbit Hash. She was born on May 4, 1838, and died on March 16, 1916. She never married. She was the daughter of James Nelson Stephens, whose father was Benjamin Stephens Jr., the family patriarch of the Boone County line. Her sister, Jane Kendall Stephens, was married to James A. Wilson, the first proprietor of the Rabbit Hash General Store. This page from her book is a collection of hand-drawn and signed calling cards of young men who apparently were enlisted in military service during the Civil War. At the time of the war, she would have been in her mid-teens. *From the Rabbit Hash Historical Society collection.*

a rather large estate to be divided among his heirs. He owned, besides the farm in East End, property in Rising Sun, Indiana, and lands and slaves in Missouri. His will is an elaborate and lengthy instrument which illustrates his desire to treat all his heirs and slaves fairly. By the time of his death, his descendants were firmly established in both Boone County and Missouri. Since that time they have spread to most of the Western states as well as Florida, Virginia, Maryland, New Jersey and Connecticut.

Like the immediate offspring of James and John Ryle, the twelve living children of Benjamin Stephens Jr. were quite prolific. Not unexpectedly, the two families intermarried frequently, to the point of first cousins marrying first cousins. Herbert Ryle explains:

In 1824, the first Stephens-Ryle marriage occurred when David Ryle married Elizabeth Stephens. Later, great grandfather, Sandy Ryle married Mary Ann Stephens, [which represented] *the youngest son of John Ryle, Jr. marrying the youngest daughter of Benjamin Stephens, Jr. Since then more than one hundred marriages have taken place between Ryle-Stephens or Stephens-Stephens or Ryle-Ryle descendants.*

A rare vintage ceramic crockery jug inscribed, "Riddell and Stephens/Dealers in Dry Goods & Groceries/Rabbitt [*sic*] Hash, Ky." Since L.L. Stephens bought out James A. Wilson's share of the business and was partners with Cal Riddell for only a few short years, there are few extant remnants of that partnership. This jug serves as an important and significant artifact of that short time in history. *Photo by Callie Clare.*

The Ryles and Stephenses have played a huge role in the commercial and economic history of the town of Rabbit Hash. After the James A. Wilson legacy, the general store was taken over by Cal Riddle, but the store remained in the Wilson family. As a matter of fact, Cal Riddle actually lived with Ben Wilson and his wife. The store's ownership changed hands in 1919, when it went from the Wilson family to the Craig family. At that point, it was generally a Craig, a Stephens or a Ryle who owned or operated the two general stores.

7

MORE THAN JUST A GENERAL STORE

Why, on Saturdays they would all meet down to the store and argue about religion, and then on Sundays, they'd stand outside the church doors and argue politics.

The store and the church. Those were the two most significant and important places in the Rabbit Hash/East Bend community. But the store overshadowed the church many times over in claiming the distinction of being the pulse of the community. The above epigraph was directly out of the mouth of Robert Haydon Wilson (November 5, 1903– May 12, 1986), the grandson of James A. Wilson, the store's first proprietor. Samuel C. Wilson (January 6, 1871–July 9, 1961) was his father, and he was always considered the "chronicler" of the area, a designation that Robert Haydon inherited and performed flawlessly. With his slow southern drawl and a nearly spent Camel growing out of the right corner of his mouth, he was the quintessential rural storyteller. And he never missed a lick. If a debate taking place behind the store's potbellied stove ended up in a draw, the solution was always: "We'll just have to ask Robert Haydon." And that was that.

There were times in the 1930 and '40s when Rabbit Hash had two and sometimes three stores in the little community. One of the stores was mainly a hardware and feed and implement store, but it still carried some of the same items sold by the other two general merchandise stores. The competing families were the Stephenses, the Ryles and the Craigs (whose daughter married a Stephens and directly competed with her brother, a Craig). There

The East Bend Baptist Church, aka the "white church," as it appears today. *Photo by Callie Clare.*

The East Bend Methodist Episcopal Church, aka the "red church," as it appears today. *Photo by Callie Clare.*

were also two churches in the community, the East Bend Baptist, which was the oldest, and the East Bend Methodist. If one had a good strong arm, he could almost hit one church from the other with a rock. The Baptist church was painted white and the Methodist church red. People would identify which church they attended by saying, "I go to the red church" or "I go to the white church." Robert Haydon clarified things in a conversation once when he explained, "Well, the folks who do business in this store, they all go to the white church, and the ones who do business in that store, they all go to the red church."

That may have been a humorous exaggeration on Haydon's part, but for some select folks, it was a true statement. Generally, the entire community was fairly close knit, and they frequented both stores and were invited to one another's church picnics and socials. But they were all buried in the same cemetery, the East Bend Methodist Cemetery, which remains the case to this day.

The Rabbit Hash General Store has always been the centerpiece of this community. The store has remained the staple around which the rest of

An interior shot of the Craig general store taken by the renowned Cincinnati photographer Paul Briol. This photo was used for the frontispiece of the 1944 book by Thomas D. Clark, *Pills, Petticoats and Plows. From author's personal collection.*

A photograph of the C.W. Craig store taken by renowned Cincinnati photographer Paul Briol while he was in Rabbit Hash in the early 1940s. *From the Rabbit Hash Historical Society collection via the Cincinnati Historical Society Paul Briol collection.*

the community evolves. It is the eyes and ears of the town. It is the soul and the conscience. It is the common denominator whereby everyone who enters through the screen door in the spring and summer or the single-paned exterior door in the fall and winter is welcomed equally and invited to hold court. No matter who comes in, they bring with them news, opinion, gossip, rumor, conjecture, lies, commentary and editorials, and they feel free to share these with others. It serves as the clearinghouse for the neighborhood's business. Nothing is sacred and beyond discussion. The topics just depend on who is present and, more often, who isn't. It has been this way for years and years.

The proprietor of the general store had always been the postmaster of Rabbit Hash. A small bank of pigeonholes was stationed on the left side of the counter as one entered. This served as the Rabbit Hash Post Office from the beginning of mail service up until the advent of Rural Route Delivery in 1913. In 1879, the postal service dictated that a name change was in order for the town. There was too much confusion and error in the delivery of the mail destined for

A Rabbit Hash postmarked letter, 1893. *From the Rabbit Hash Historical Society collection.*

Carlton but ending up in Carrollton and vice versa. So Rabbit Hash received its officially sanctioned name and its own postmark to prove it, even though the locals had been calling the place Rabbit Hash for about thirty years.

Robert Haydon Wilson once told a reporter by the name of Byron Crawford, from the Louisville, Kentucky newspaper the *Courier Journal*, when asked to explain the origin of the town's name, that wild rabbits were always abundant around the area. "Back when I was a kid," he added, "during the late teens, if you was any kind of shot at all, you could go out and kill anywhere from 20 to 35 rabbits in a day's time." Crawford also noted that "the Rabbit Hash General Store in those days paid anywhere from 15 cents to 25 cents apiece for the rabbits, Wilson said, and often one of its storerooms would be filled with gunny sacks full of rabbits, waiting to be shipped to Cincinnati, where they were sold for food." What Wilson neglected to tell the reporter was that once skinned and cleaned, a rabbit carcass didn't look that much different from the carcass of a cat, and several of the lads who were poorer shots in the neighborhood saw to it that many a feral cat found its way to some of the finer Cincinnati eateries.

Reuben Gold Thwaites was a noted historian and director of the Wisconsin Historical Society. In the spring and summer of 1894, he embarked on a 1,100-mile adventure in a fifteen-foot wooden rowboat, along with his wife, their ten-year-old son and his wife's brother. They traveled down the Monongahela from Brownsville, Pennsylvania, to the mouth of the Ohio

River at Pittsburgh and then on down the entire 981-mile length of the Ohio. He wanted a firsthand experience of traveling along the same rivers and landscape that the early settlers themselves had experienced. He kept a handwritten and photographic journal of his trip. His Kodak camera took black-and-white round photographs. The front cover of this book features photos he took while in Rabbit Hash, Kentucky. He published his journal in book form in 1897, with the title *Afloat on the Ohio*, and republished it in 1903 as *On the Storied Ohio.* On page 189 he writes:

A section of the 1883 D.J. Lake & Co. *Atlas of Boone, Kenton and Campbell Counties, Kentucky*, showing the Rabbit Hash portion of the Carlton Magisterial District. *Courtesy of the Boone County Public Library collection.*

> *Rabbit Hash, Ky. (502 miles), is a crude hamlet of a hundred souls, lying nestled in a green amphitheater. A horse-power ferry runs over to the larger village of Rising Sun, its Indiana neighbor. There is a small general store in Rabbit Hash, with post office and paint-shop attachment, and nearby a tobacco warehouse and a blacksmith shop, with a few cottages scattered at intervals over the bottom. The postmaster, who is also the storekeeper and painter, greeted me with joy, as I deposited with him mail-matter bearing eighteen cents' worth of stamps; for his is one of those offices where the salary is the value of the stamps cancelled. It is not every day that so liberal a patron comes along.*
>
> *"Jemimi! Bill! but guv'm'nt business 's look'n up—there'll be some o' th' rest o' us a-want'n this yere off'c, a'ter nex' 'lection, I reck'n"*
>
> *It was the blacksmith, who is also the ferryman, who thus bantered the delighted postmaster—a broad-faced, big-chested, brown-armed man, with his neck-muscles standing out like cords, and his mild blue eyes dancing with fun, the rustic disciple of Tubal Cain. He sat just without the door, leather apron on, and red shirt-sleeves rolled up, playing checkers on an upturned soap-box, with a jolly fat farmer from the hill-country, whose broad straw hat was cocked on the back of his bald head. The merry laughter of the two was infectious. The half-dozen spectators, small farmers whose teams and saddle-horses were hitched to the postoffice railing, were themselves hilarious over the game; and a saffron-skinned, hollow-cheeked woman in a blue sun-bonnet, with a market-basket over her arm, stopped for a moment at the threshold to look on, and then passed within the store, her eyes having caught the merriment, although her facial muscles had apparently lost their power of smiling.*
>
> *Joining the little company, I found that the farmer was a blundering player, but made up in fun what he lacked in science. I tried to ascertain the origin of the name Rabbit Hash, as applied to the hamlet. Everyone had a different opinion, evidently invented on the spur of the moment, but all 'lowed that none but the tobacco agent could tell, and he was off in the country for the day; as for themselves, they had, they confessed, never thought of it before. It always had been Rabbit Hash and like enough would be to the end of time.*

From the sound of this journal description, the Rabbit Hash locals were playing the very same role back in 1894 that Callie Clare stressed in her recent work, *Potions & Notions: The Legacy of Rabbit Hash, Kentucky* (2011), which was to give to visitors and strangers to their town the very stereotypical characters they were looking for and expecting; that is, the socially inferior, simpleton, laissez-faire, country bumpkins who in reality were sly like foxes.

Besides this knack for politely excluding strangers from the "real meaning of Rabbit Hash" and disguising the secrets that would make any normal, ordinary, decent, God-fearing person want to become part of this rare and uniquely quasi-utopia, the local residents could also open their hearts and souls to newcomers. But of course, they first had to pass admission criteria—a hierarchy of ascending levels of requirements and tests—and then be voted on and approved unanimously by the board of governors. The pledge(s) would then be invited to sit behind the potbellied stove in the general store and ceremoniously gifted with knowledge of all the "secrets" of the membership. It was not at all unlike the procedure necessary to be accepted into the International Order of Freemasonry, the Knights of Pythius, the Grange Association or the Modern Woodmen of America.

This particular function of the general store still holds true to this day. Back in 1978, the town of Rabbit Hash was literally "circling the drain." The collection of original commercial structures was quickly falling into a dangerous state of neglect and ill repair. The lack of river-related economy and commerce and the shift from small community business to that of suburban super shopping malls resulting from updated and well-maintained state and federal highways, along with state-of-the-art motor vehicles and inexpensive gasoline prices, rang the death knell for the town of Rabbit Hash, Kentucky. This is when thirty-eight-year-old Lowell L. Scott stepped in and, within several years, singlehandedly orchestrated the purchase of every building and piece of property in the two-and-a-half-acre Rabbit Hash proper. His goal was to stop the decay and neglect and bring the town back to the standard he had enjoyed as a child. It was not an easy task, but he succeeded. The real proof of his success was not when the general store reopened as a legitimate mercantile again but when, one day, Louie was approached by one of the skeptical "speakers of the house" who happened to be holding court behind the stove in the store. He approached Louie and, with a slight smile, announced, "Louie, looks like you took this entire town without even firing a shot!" The old-timers were glad to have their social center and gathering place back again. The store reclaimed its spot in the neighborhood as the centerpiece of the town and the social clearinghouse with its finger once again on the pulse of the community.

It is agreeably a much-overused cliché now, but what an invaluable aid to history and historians it would be "if only these walls could talk." Imagine what the general store walls could tell us! In February 1836, was there

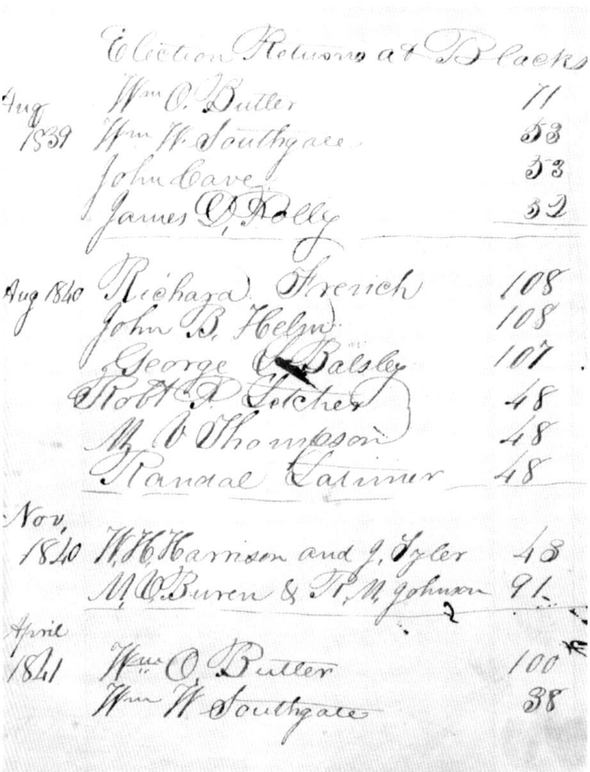

Election Returns at Blacks

Aug 1839	Wm O. Butler	71
	Wm W. Southgate	53
	John Cave	53
	James [illegible] Kelly	32
Aug 1840	Richard French	108
	John B. Helm	108
	George [illegible] Balsley	107
	Robt A. Fletcher	48
	M. C. Thompson	48
	Randal Latimer	48
Nov, 1840	W. H. Harrison and J. Tyler	48
	M. V. Buren & R. M. Johnson	71
April 1841	Wm O. Butler	100
	Wm W. Southgate	38

A page from James A. Wilson's Constable Day Book reporting election results from his magisterial district. Note the presidential election results of November 1840 near the bottom. William Henry Harrison and John Tyler received a total of forty-eight votes, while Martin Van Buren and Richard Mentor Johnson received seventy-one votes. Of course, Harrison actually won the presidency over incumbent Van Buren, but he was in office a little over one month before his death, with John Tyler assuming the reins of commander in chief. (Richard M. Johnson was a nephew of Cave Johnson, a prominent Boone Countian). *From the Rabbit Hash Historical Society collection.*

anybody sitting by the stove talking about the battle for the Alamo taking place in Texas? In March 1837, were they discussing the inauguration of President Martin Van Buren and his vice president, Richard M. Johnson, who had strong Boone County ties as a cousin to North Bend's Cave Johnson and even owned property in the county? Did the global economic crisis that came to a head in May as the Panic of 1837 really have any kind of impact on anyone in Rabbit Hash to the point that they would feel a need to discuss it?

In April 1841, was anyone saddened or shocked to hear of the death of recently elected President William Henry Harrison from pneumonia after only one month in office. Surely this was big news in the small river town since Harrison was from North Bend, Ohio, just upriver from Rabbit Hash. Perhaps there was speculation and discussion about the possibility and plausibility of some Ryle or Stephens family member who had earlier immigrated to Missouri being a member of the very first organized wagon train leaving there and heading for the Oregon Territory. In December 1845, was somebody asking, "What's this thing I heard about called the

Monroe Doctrine and what exactly is Manifest Destiny?" Or perhaps in 1846, these walls heard someone ask, "Did you hear that we declared war on Mexico?" How many families discussed having members in that war? Surely there were conversations about the Trail of Tears and the U.S. policies about Native American displacement. After all, a lot of them knew Silas Dinsmoor from upriver at Belleview. Dinsmoor lived in Belleview Bottoms (Grant) and actually farmed Lochry's Island. He had just passed away and was buried up on the hill behind his nephew James Dinsmore's house. He worked for many years as an Indian agent for the government and was always fair and friendly to these Native Americans and highly concerned about their treatment from the government. Was anyone upset to hear that a group of Mormons was being forced out of Illinois because of violent clashes against their religious beliefs and being led to Salt Lake City in Utah Territory under the leadership of Brigham Young? After all, wasn't our country founded on the principles of religious freedom?

Just imagine the heated discussions and disagreements that took place in this general store during the decade of the 1850s as the question of slavery reared its ugly head once and for all in the public arena and started breathing fire and shooting flames into our national conscience, affecting everything of a domestic, human, religious, moral, political, economical and physical nature. Discussions and conversations about Harriet Beecher Stowe's *Uncle Tom's Cabin*, released in 1851, had to be frequent. Not everyone owned a copy, but before too long, everyone had heard about the book and had formed their own opinions. Doomed to become the unfortunate border state, Kentucky and Kentuckians found themselves caught in the line of fire of this fire-breathing monster, and none more so than the residents of Boone County. Most of the area farmers were slaveholders—at least the more successful farmers and landowners were. But they always bragged about being the benevolent slave owners of the times. Somehow those two words contradicted each other—a semantic dichotomy, and a very thought-provoking one, fueling, no doubt, some heated discussions within those general store walls.

Besides *Uncle Tom's Cabin*, the neighborhood residents also had another major publication to peruse, study, quote and argue. This happened to be written by a local citizen named Henry Field James ("of Kentucky"), quite possibly from Rising Sun, Indiana, but supposedly living somewhere just above the mouth of Big Bone Creek (Mile #514.6). The publication was entitled *Abolitionism Unveiled; or Its Origin, Progress, and Pernicious Tendency Fully Developed.* If only these wall could talk!

8
FROM STEAMBOAT TO AEROPLANE

Throughout the early history of Rabbit Hash, it was not uncommon to either witness or hear about a steamboat wreck or some other river-related boat disaster. It just went with the territory. But on Friday, August 11, 1944, as Reuben Kirtley was out in his East Bend Bottoms fields working with his tractor, he witnessed something very much out of the ordinary. An odd, eerie noise overpowered the sound of his tractor motor, causing him to look up just as a huge U.S. military C-47 aircraft went over his head and crash-landed right in the middle of his wheat field across the creek from where he was working. After some tense moments of fancy handling and maneuvering by the pilot, the plane finally came to rest after an abrupt ninety-degree turn kept it from entering both the Ohio River and the mouth of nearby Lick Creek, which joins the Ohio at Kirtley's Landing at Mile #512.0. On this day, "Kirtley Landing" took on a whole new meaning.

After the aircraft came to a complete halt, Reuben watched as two uniformed crewmen emerged from the wreck, apparently unharmed. Both of the propellers were missing, and the fuselage had a gaping tear in it. It was not made known where the plane was headed, nor was its mission revealed. It was all top secret, and the crew members were not allowed to give out any information. Everything was classified. However, the fact that it happened right there in Reuben Kirtley's wheat field did not remain a secret. The spectacle drew quite a crowd of neighbors and onlookers over the next few days.

An unidentified local newspaper clipping revealed that there were three men aboard—the pilot and co-pilot and a navigator—and they were not

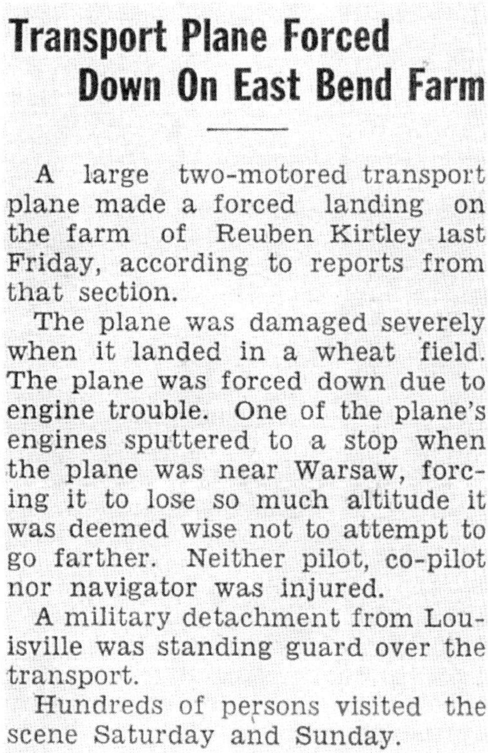

Transport Plane Forced Down On East Bend Farm

A large two-motored transport plane made a forced landing on the farm of Reuben Kirtley last Friday, according to reports from that section.

The plane was damaged severely when it landed in a wheat field. The plane was forced down due to engine trouble. One of the plane's engines sputtered to a stop when the plane was near Warsaw, forcing it to lose so much altitude it was deemed wise not to attempt to go farther. Neither pilot, co-pilot nor navigator was injured.

A military detachment from Louisville was standing guard over the transport.

Hundreds of persons visited the scene Saturday and Sunday.

Right: A local newspaper reporting on the military transport plane that went down in East Bend Bottoms in 1944. *From the Rabbit Hash Historical Society collection (donated by Betty Kirtly).*

Below: Reuben Kirtly posing alongside the wrecked military transport plane that went down in his wheat field as he was working in an adjacent field. 1944. *From the Rabbit Hash Historical Society collection (donated by Betty Kirtly).*

allowed to leave the plane. Armed with sidearms, they were to guard the plane at all times but could not reveal the reason for the secrecy. It was later discovered that this particular military plane was equipped with an experimental newly developed and very sophisticated radar device in its nose cone. This plane happened to be a military prototype.

A five-man salvage crew was deployed to the East Bend Bottoms site from Bowman's Field in Louisville to dismantle and retrieve the plane and all its parts and haul it back to Louisville. This was no minor task. They had to first pump out all the fuel into barrels and then remove the wings and load the plane, the wings, all the miscellaneous components and the barrels of fuel onto trucks. To top that off, they had to do it all in the middle of a farmer's field right next to the Ohio River.

One of the members of the recovery team was Roland Rogers. Back in 2001, he was living in California. It just so happened that Louie Scott, at that time the sole owner of the town of Rabbit Hash, had made up his mind to find out more about the plane crash that he vividly remembered as a four-year-old child. He had visited the site every day with his father in a Model A Ford, in which he traveled "shotgun" by standing on the

Fuel from the wrecked military transport plane was the first chore of recovery and had to be hand pumped from the plane and collected into barrels on this military flatbed trailer. *From the Rabbit Hash Historical Society collection (donated by Betty Kirtly).*

passenger's side floor, clinging to the windshield frame. He remembered how much excitement and activity the event had generated in the Rabbit Hash/East Bend neighborhood at the time. And then, just as suddenly as it stirred up everybody's interest and curiosity, after the few days it took to remove the wreckage—that was it. He didn't recall ever hearing any more about it.

So Louie got on the Internet and researched numerous military and aircraft-related sites, just putting out the question of whether anyone anywhere knew about this crash-landing of a military C-47 in 1944 in Boone County, Kentucky.

Sure enough, he was contacted by octogenarian Roland Rogers, who clearly remembered the recovery mission. He and four other men were dispatched to drive the one hundred miles from Bowman Field to East Bend Bottoms in a military truck with a sixty-foot trailer, a crane truck and a jeep to dismantle the aircraft and bring it back. They were supplied with all the necessary tools and equipment to see the job through. Rogers recalled operating the jeep to knock down trees and other obstructions in their paths. They were instructed to bring along enough provisions to last five to seven days, and their orders explicitly pointed out that they were to sleep in the fuselage with the crew and to provide round-the-clock armed security.

Norman Schwenke, a neighboring East Bend farmer, remembered the event vividly and perhaps a bit differently. He related that the armed guards and secretive atmosphere ended every evening when the local farmers would all drive up to Elsmere together with the military crew for beers and food.

When the plane was finally loaded on trucks and ready to go, the recovery team had to clear the road of all trees and other obstructions, like telephone poles and mailboxes. The width of the loaded truck and trailer was twenty-four feet across, and the narrow, graveled country roads were no more than eighteen feet wide. They were forced to return to Bowman Field via a roundabout and out-of-the-way circuitous route through Frankfort in order to utilize the few bridges that would accommodate their cargo. The chore of replacing mailboxes and phone poles was left to the locals; the military never returned after that last day on the site. After all, these were war times! Who was going to complain to the U.S. military?

All her life, Betty Kirtley still wondered why they just didn't load the plane and all its parts onto a down-bound barge and float it back to Louisville. For sure, it would have been a lot easier on Boone County's utilities and infrastructure!

Elizabeth (Betty) Kirtley was Reuben's wife. She joined the Internet researchers Louie Scott and Roland Rogers in search of more answers about the mysterious military air crash in East Bend Bottoms close to sixty years prior. Roland remembered Betty vividly because she prepared breakfast every morning for the demolition team and the aircrew. He remembered the big farm bell clanging to let them know the food was ready and their immediate Pavlovian responses of dropping the tools right then and there and beating it to the farmhouse at the other end of the fields.

Roland Rogers recorded in his written account:

> *The first load out of the field was the salvaged gasoline. The fuel was pumped out of the airplane tanks into the drums sitting on the small truck bed. The truck was parked on a wide dirt area where two small roads crossed near the town of Florence, Kentucky. The gasoline drum area was roped off in an attempt to keep the public away from the drums and gasoline fumes. I believe it was on a week-end when I was guarding the gasoline, when a woman slipped under the rope barrier to get a closer look. She was smoking a cigarette, and those of us standing nearby shouted at her to get out of there because of the 100 octane aviation fuel in the drums.*
>
> *As the larger parts were loaded, the trucks and trailers were left parked in the farmer's field. In maneuvering the Jeep, I backed it past the loaded outer wing panels. A corner of the windshield caught the mounting flange on the undamaged wing, bending the wing flange and bending the windshield frame of the Jeep, plus breaking the windshield. Our crew leader made no comment, but I was very nervous about it. What would happen when we returned to Bowman Field? (Nothing happened; I might as well have broken a lead pencil.)*
>
> *Now we were all ready to go, but go which way with that 24-foot wide load? The crew leader took the Jeep out on a scouting trip to check out the various bridges and other possible obstructions. It was found we could not return by the same route we used traveling from Bowman Field. A roundabout way through Frankfort was selected. Although not a fully clear route, it was the best we could do.*
>
> *When we were all ready to leave the farmer's field, I used the Jeep to break down several small saplings, making a path for the trucks and trailers. As we moved from the field onto the country road, we became aware of many other overlooked obstacles. First, there were many mailboxes set close to the edge of the road which were in the way. The jeep quickly pushed them over, breaking the mounting posts. We were traveling over a very narrow graveled road. Our load was 24 feet wide, and the road was maybe 18 feet wide at the most. A few large trees and many small ones had to be cut, as well as telephone poles. Anything in our way had to go. Cars coming toward*

us were forced into the ditch to clear our wide load. This width was the result of having the C-47 center wing section (and fuselage) on a trailer.

Louie Scott (four years old at the time of the wreck) remembers this much very clearly:

And yes…I do remember you fellas taking the plane out the road to Burlington and totally destroying the only paved road in these parts. [Laughs] *Well ya did…Now you mention having a damn jeep…that is so ironic…see, I am 4 years old, 4 ½ maybe, the day you were moving it…My father and myself were just being nosey and in the way typical of locals for ya I am sure.* [Laughs] *We were on that gravel road, maybe 2 tenths of a mile from the crash site…We are in a model A ford…I remember I was standing on the passenger side floor, as I always did. I was just overwhelmed by the size of all those pieces. I remember the truck with the wing on it I think…It was approximately 10 o'clock in the morning… dates…no clue here. My dad was terribly in the way in this damn Model A bomb.* [Laughs] *One of your guys had motioned us to get the hell outta the way and I remember dad drove the A bomb off into the ditch. Lo and behold here comes some wild man in a damn jeep…runs the jeep up on the bank…a fella jumps out with an axe…runs over to a telephone pole and proceeds to just cut it down. I remember my dad was just astounded that he cut the pole down. He just knew that someone was in trouble for that trick.* [Laughs] *Could have been you were in that jeep? My mind is racing for sure…I can still hear those wires sing as that pole fell…twing… twang…and can remember the sunlight reflecting off that copper…see… this business was all new to me. I knew then…this thing was coming out of there…made no difference what you encountered. You guys moving stuff…and I remember the atmosphere there where the guy cut the pole down…a lot of hollerin…screaming…get it done…stop at nothing…we are movin'. You guys were hell bent for sure…then…in my small mind… ya disappeared and I went back to diggin' fish worms. But all that stuck in my mind all these years…fantastic."*

Roland Rogers added this to the story:

Further down the road we had a more difficult time. We had come to the most challenging part of our journey. On the edge of this town was a bridge with sides so high it blocked the big rig. The 60-foot trailer had to be raised a considerable amount for the load to pass over this bridge. To accomplish this, the 25-foot trailer was unloaded, and the AutoCar was detached from the long trailer. Then the crane, which was traveling with us, lifted the rear of the 60-foot trailer (and load) until the 25-foot trailer could be backed under the rear wheels of the 60-foot trailer. The crane then was positioned at the front of the 60-foot trailer to raise that end to the correct height. With the crane leading and pulling the 60-foot trailer and its load, and the 25-foot trailer and its truck operating backward, it successfully crossed the bridge as one unit. I noticed we exceeded the bridge capacity by a large percentage.

It took quite a bit of time to accomplish the movement of the big load across the bridge. Police cars had blocked the road, but still one civilian got through. The policeman from one car was in a nearby coffee shop, and I sat in the driver's seat of the car, studying the emergency equipment. A button on the floor was a mystery to me, but I thought it might be the switch for the siren. The car that got through our road block came around a curve at a rapid speed and was quite near. I hit the floor button with my foot, and yes, it was for the siren. I'm not sure which was the quickest, the renegade car stopping or the police officer coming out of the coffee shop to see who was playing with his car.

A pilot peering out of the cockpit of the wrecked C-47 military transport plane while a local farm truck investigates the scene in 1944. *From the Rabbit Hash Historical Society collection (donated by Betty Kirtly).*

There was just one more hair raising situation. As we crept through Frankfort at a walking pace, a large group of people followed us on foot. I was near the front of the 60-foot trailer watching for tree branches, overhead wires, etc., that might get in the way of our progress. I turned to look toward the back of the load, and froze. I couldn't shout a warning, or give any sign of a pending disaster. When the engines were removed from the wing, the exhaust pipe was separated so that what was attached to the engine went with the engine. The remaining exhaust pipe extension stayed attached to the firewall and center wing section. This was formed from thin stainless steel. It was essentially a thin walled pipe about eight or ten inches in diameter. It had an essentially knife edge facing forward. As I looked back, I saw a man standing in front of the slowly moving unit and facing me. He did not see the exhaust pipe extension coming toward him. I could see his head was in direct line with the pipe, and it looked like his head might fit into the pipe. The pipe was about to become a circular guillotine. It all happened so fast there was no time to take any action.

I will leave you, dear reader, with the fact that the man moved just in time to avoid being decapitated. The rest of the trip was uneventful.

9
CONCLUSION AND WHAT THE FUTURE HOLDS

Probably the most important and significant revival of the town of Rabbit Hash occurred in 1978. The town was clearly on its last leg and literally "circling the drain." Lib and Cliff Stephens ran the general store at the time, and they could hear the death knell ringing every morning. They were frustrated and angry. Lib drove the county school bus to supplement their meager income from the general store. There were no other businesses in the town. Demolition "by neglect" was showing its ugly face and becoming so familiar that the daily downhill changes were no longer recognized.

Enter Lowell Lee Scott, or Louie, as the Rabbit Hash/East Bend neighborhood knew Jewell and Sally Scott's son, born, raised, educated and invested in Rabbit Hash. Invested in that he recognized the fact that a Boone County historic treasure and culturally iconic Ohio River hamlet was about to succumb to the same fate that the rest of the town had suffered in the 1937 flood. Louie purchased the Ryle Brothers' Feed and Seed store across the road from Lib and Cliff's Rabbit Hash General Store. Louie began to stabilize the structure and bring it back to a viable commercial property. "It was like scraping shit off a turd," he would say in describing his efforts to save a part of the beloved town of his youth. But he persevered and stabilized the structure, giving it a new life as a woodworking shop and later adding a wood stove manufactory.

Eventually, Lib and Cliff trolled the opportunity to Louie for the general store for a similar resurrection project, and he eventually struck and took the bait. He purchased the original Rabbit Hash General Store and its contents and helped keep it in continuous operation (since its opening in 1831) while sleeping on a rollaway bed next to the stove every night. But his sacrifice paid off. The town of Rabbit Hash was given new life and one more chance to meet a new generation.

Cliff Stephens, son-in-law of C.W. Craig, clerked in the store after his return home from serving in World War II and eventually became owner and proprietor until it was last sold in 1978. Photo dated 1970. *From the Rabbit Hash Historical Society collection.*

Monopoly-like, Louie eventually purchased every parcel in the town proper, amounting to about three acres and five buildings, until he was the sole owner of Rabbit Hash, Kentucky. Over the years, his blood, sweat and tears (and money) stabilized and rejuvenated the small Ohio River town, and the name Rabbit Hash promoted and marketed itself without any additional effort on Louie's part. The town is now owned by the Rabbit Hash Historical Society, a 501(c)3 nonprofit organization and is "alive and well." All of the seven buildings in the town have been restored and adapted to commercial reuse, thus sustaining the necessary funds to maintain these same buildings according to the National Register standards as mandated by the Department of Interior and the National Park Service.

Today, the town and all the structures are in pretty good shape. But it hasn't been an easy job. When attempting to maintain an all-wooden town that sits literally twenty feet from a major inland waterway in the humid Ohio River Valley, it takes proactive planning strategies and comprehensive maintenance schedules just to keep it afloat, so to speak. The other necessary ingredient in this mix is money. And plenty of it!

There are a lot of tools in the Rabbit Hash preservation toolbox. Benefitting from a variety of local, state and federal preservation programs, Rabbit Hash has been fortunate enough to qualify for some small grants

A National Register Historic District marker. *Photo by Callie Clare. Courtesy of the Rabbit Hash Historical Society.*

and tax benefits, as well as some prestigious designations in the national historic preservation movement. Most notably, the town is designated a National Register Historic District, as well as a Preserve America Community. But these achievements carry no financial benefits. The bricks-and-mortar funding needed to keep the town going comes from the same place any other labor of love does—hard work and thinking outside the box.

What makes Rabbit Hash so viable is adaptive reuse. Every structure in town has been adapted to a commercial use other than its intended purpose. The general store is still the gathering place of the community, but it is no longer the place to pick up the mail or purchase patent medicine, hog rings or fabric. It is the place to visit and have a snack, soft drink or beer; buy gifts, trinkets and organic food; and listen to live roots music behind the wood stove. The ironworks is no longer the place to buy hardware or woodstoves. Now it serves as a wine shop and tasting room as well as a bed-and-breakfast. The blacksmith shop is an antiques store, and the doctor's office is now the headquarters for a cultural resource management and archaeology firm.

There is a huge difference between a mothballed historic structure that is merely an antique artifact within a museum and one that has been rejuvenated and given new life and purpose. The vibrancy of reuse adds another layer of health and protection to the place and secures its future.

The transition of this significant little historic Ohio River town from the former status of "circling the drain" into the "alive and well" 100 percent occupancy historic tourism destination that it is today speaks volumes for investing and taking pride in one's historic and cultural past. Depending on the mood and whims of *La Belle Rivière*, Rabbit Hash will survive and be around for a long time.

BIBLIOGRAPHY

Banta, R.E. *The Ohio.* Rivers of America Books. New York: Rinehart & Company, 1949.

Boone County Clerk. Ferry Keepers Bonds, Ferry Covenants, Deed Books. Boone County Courthouse, Old Records Room.

Boone County Recorder. Microfilm, 1875 to Present. Boone County Public Library.

Cauffield, Joyce V.B., and Carolyn E. Banfield, eds. *The River Book: Cincinnati and the Ohio.* Cincinnati, OH: The Program for Cincinnati, 1981.

Cincinnati Enquirer. "Rabbit Hash…Stores, Stories and Pot-Bellied Stove." August 15, 1963.

Cincinnati Pictorial Enquirer. "They Call It Rabbit Hash." October 10, 1954.

Cincinnati Times Star. "10 Wet Days." A Pictorial History of 1937 Greater Cincinnati Flood. Published by the *Cincinnati Times-Star* for the benefit of the American Red Cross, 1937.

Clare, Callie. *Potions & Notions: The Legacy of Rabbit Hash, Kentucky.* Covington, KY: The Merlot Group, 2011.

Clare, Callie, Caitlyn Clare and Donald Clare Jr. "The History of Rabbit Hash." In *Ancestry: Our Ohio River Heritage.* Mt. Vernon, IN: Windmill Publications, Inc., 1996.

Clare, Donald E. Draft of Nomination for Rabbit Hash, Kentucky. National Register of Historic Places, Fall 1995.

Clark, Thomas D. *A History of Kentucky.* Lexington, KY: John Bradford Press, 1960.

———. *Pills, Petticoats and Plows: The Southern Country Store.* New York: Bobbs-Merrill Company, 1944.

Collins, Lewis. *History of Kentucky.* 2 vols. Frankfort: Kentucky Historical Society, 1874.

Conrad, William, ed. *Boone County: The Top of Kentucky, 1792–1992.* A Project of Kentucky's 200th Anniversary. Boone County Committee. Fort Mitchell, KY: Picture This! Books, 1992.

Cramer, Zadok. *The Navigator.* 8th ed. Ann Arbor, MI: University Microfilms, Inc., 1966.

Crisman, Kevin J., and Arthur B. Cohn. *When Horses Walked on Water: Horse-Powered Ferries in Nineteenth-Century America.* Washington, D.C.: Smithsonian Institution Press, 1998.

Dayton Daily News. "Rabbit Hash Isn't Just a Town, It's a Way of Life." July 29, 1984.

De Chambrun, Clara Longworth. *Cincinnati: Story of the Queen City.* New York: Charles Scribner's Sons, 1939.

Dichtl, William. *Ohio County Indiana.* Images of America. Chicago: Arcadia Publishing, 2001.

Filson, John. *Discovery, Settlement, and Present State of Kentucke.* New York: Corinth Books, 1784.

Firestone, Clark B. *Sycamore Shores.* New York: Robert M. McBride & Company, 1936.

Fitzgerald, William, and Anne Fitzgerald. *John Calvert's Notebook: Containing Data on the Stephens, Ryle and Related Families of Boone County, Kentucky.* Florence, KY: self-published, 1955.

Fowke, Gerard. *The Evolution of the Ohio River.* Indianapolis, IN: Hollenback Press, 1933.

Hudson, Karen. "Identifying and Documenting the Kentucky Boxed House." *Heritage Sprint Supplement* 1, no. 3 (April–May 1992).

Hunter, David. "Drive Around Boone County Re-Discovers Rabbit Hash, Kentucky." *Cincinnati Enquirer*, May 11, 1975.

Hutslar, Donald A. *The Architecture of Migration: Log Construction in the Ohio Country, 1750–1850.* Athens: Ohio University Press, 1986.

Jones, R.R. *The Ohio River: Charts, Drawings, and Descriptions of Features Affecting Navigation.* Washington, D.C.: United States Government Printing Office. 1929.

Klein, Benjamin, and Eleanor Klein, eds. *The Ohio River Handbook and Picture Album.* Cincinnati, OH: Young and Klein, Inc., 1950.

Lake, D.J. & Co. *An Atlas of Boone, Kenton And Campbell Counties, Kentucky: From Actual Surveys under the Direction of B.N. Griffing.* Philadelphia: D.J. Lake & Co., 1883.

Nelson, William H. *The Buried Treasure: A Rabbit Hash Mystery.* 1890. Reprint, Mt. Vernon, IN: Windmill Publications, Inc., 1997.

Perkins, George Gilpin. *A Kentucky Judge.* Washington, D.C.: W.F. Roberts Company, 1931.

Perrin, W.H., J.H. Battle and G.C. Kniffen. *Kentucky: A History of the State.* 7th ed. Louisville, KY: F.A. Battery and Company, 1887.

Personal and oral history interviews with Wanetta Clause, Sally Scott, Bill Stephens, Lib Stephens and Robert Haydon Wilson. 1979–1990s.

Rising Sun and Ohio County Sesquicentennial, Inc. *Rising Sun and Ohio County Sesquicentennial, July 5 11, 1964.* Rising Sun, IN, 1964.

Rogers, Roland. "Reuben Kirtley Had More than Grain in His Wheat Field/C-47 Airplane…Picking Up the Pieces." Unpublished ms., 2001.

Ryle, Herbert E. *The Stephens/Ryle Book: The History and Descendants of Benjamin Stephens, Sr., of Orange County, Virginia and Campbell County, Ky. and John Ryle, Sr., of Anson County, North Carolina, Who Died in 1777 and Whose Children Settled in Boone County, Kentucky.* Upper Marlboro, MD: self-published, 1988.

Ryle, Russell G. *Ohio River Images: Cincinnati to Louisville in the Packet Boat Era.* Images of America. Chicago: Arcadia Publishing, 2000.

Schrage, Robert, and Donald Clare. *Along the Ohio River: Cincinnati to Louisville.* Images of America, Postcard History Series. Chicago: Arcadia Publishing, 2006.

Shaffer, James F. *Piatt's Landing East Bend.* Prepared by the Cincinnati Gas and Electric Company General Engineering Department. Cincinnati, OH: Cincinnati Gas and Electric Company, 1978.

Thwaites, Reuben Gold. *Afloat on the Ohio.* Chicago: Way & Williams, 1897.

Wilson, James A. Collection of obituaries and family history in permanent bound family remembrances book from the Wilson family. Rabbit Hash, Kentucky.

———. Constable's Day Books. A personal record book kept by Constable James A. Wilson. Rabbit Hash, KY, 1837.

———. *Rising Sun Ferry Ledger.* Handwritten account by James A. Wilson. Rabbit Hash, KY, 1847.

Worrel, Stephen W., MA, and Anne W. Fitzgerald, BS. *Boone County, Kentucky Cemeteries.* Falls Church, VA: self-published, 1996.

———. *Boone County, Kentucky County Court Orders, 1799–1815.* Falls Church, VA: self-published, 1994.

Yealey, A.M. *History of Boone County Kentucky/Reprint of Articles Published in Newspapers Over a Period of Fifty Years.* Florence, KY: William Fitzgerald, 1960.

ABOUT THE AUTHOR

Donald Clare lives in the East Bend neighborhood of Rabbit Hash, Kentucky, with his wife, Sue, and their two daughters. By profession, he is an emergency room registered nurse. He's used to patching up booboos and treating afflicting ailments, just like those the old town was suffering back in 1978, when his friend, Louie Scott, purchased his first building in Rabbit Hash. Clare was on hand as Louie cleaned out the contents of the old feed store that was owned by his uncle. "Louie, you can't throw that out. It's historical!"

Scott simply replied, "OK, Clare. I'll throw the stuff out, and you be in charge of getting out what's historical." Jokingly, the Rabbit Hash Historical Society was formed that very night by the two of them. Now, thirty-four years later, the town of Rabbit Hash is owned and preserved by that very same society.

Clare serves as the current president of the nonprofit 501(c)3 organization. He is also a board member of the Boone County Historic Preservation Review Board and the Friends of Big Bone. He enjoys researching local history and writing articles and books about local Boone County, Kentucky, and the regional northern Kentucky area.